# A Bon Vivant's
## COOKBOOK

# A Bon Vivant's
# COOKBOOK

## A COLLECTION OF
## FINE FOREIGN AND AMERICAN RECIPES

William Templeton Veach

*with*

Helen Evans Brown

*with illustrations by*

ISADORE SELTZER

LITTLE, BROWN AND COMPANY · BOSTON · TORONTO

*Published simultaneously in Canada
by Little, Brown & Company (Canada) Limited*

PRINTED IN THE UNITED STATES OF AMERICA

*To*
*Helen de Young Cameron*
*and Whitney Warren,*
*two most wonderful friends throughout the years*

*Pour un homme riche, le plus bien rôle*
*en ce monde est celui d'Amphitryon.*

(For the man who can afford it, the most agreeable role
in the world is that of an Amphitryon.)

— GRIMOD DE LA REYNIÈRE

# Preface

THIS BOOK is a result of all the exquisite meals William Templeton Veach has served his guests. It is the kind of book that will stimulate a good cook's imagination and inspire a mediocre cook to better things. The recipes, collected by Mr. Veach for close to half a century, are as varied as one would expect from someone brought up in the gastronomically superior city of San Francisco, who later spent many years in India, then in Italy, and who is now a resident of France.

The manuscript, as I received it, was fascinating. Some of the recipes were mere ideas but worth noting, others were in European measurements — grams and liters and kilos — and still others were in the language of the experienced cook — a little of this, enough of that, cook as usual . . . But (and this is why I took on the job of preparing the manuscript) many of them were very unusual, and all were worthwhile; I thought them too good to be lost to future kings and queens of the kitchen. I have always considered that any cookbook containing even *one* fresh idea was deserving of shelf space — here was a book that was bulging with them!

HELEN EVANS BROWN

*Pasadena, California*

# Introduction

TO INTRODUCE the authors of this book is a pleasure indeed. Both are old friends. Helen Evans Brown and I have shared the authorship of a book and uncounted hours of good eating; I have shared many good dishes with Bill Veach also and now share his pride as he enters the ranks of professional cookery.

Over a period of twenty years I have visited Bill in France and Italy. I have marketed with him, helped him plan meals, and watched him prepare them. He is that rare person, an imaginative and creative cook, who takes joy in adapting recipes friends have given him, embellishing a dish he has read about, or coming up with an entirely new conception. I recall the delight with which he announced, on one of my visits to France, that he was offering me an original dish — crêpes de jambon James Beard. He had worked at the recipe during the long winter months when it was not pleasant to wander very far from his enchanting little cottage in the Sarthe.

Bill likes good company and likes to entertain. In the years when he wintered in Florence, it was his pleasure to offer luncheon to his friends once or twice a week and tea at least once a week. This was done with great style in surroundings of impeccable taste. Bill's sense of arranging a menu and presenting food is as refined as his palate. I remember particularly one Christmas I spent with him in Florence. We planned the meals for the next few days and then spent a full morning shopping in the enormous market. This was especially enjoyable to me, since it had been decided that later I should merely sit on the kitchen sidelines and watch Bill prepare our meals. My host proved to be as exacting a shopper as he is a cook. I have a clear memory of standing on the coldest stones in Florence while a fishmonger shelled each and every scampi for Bill. And certainly we squeezed every turkey in the market before finding one that satisfied Bill's knowing fingers. The winning bird was hung outside the kitchen window for two days before it was stuffed and cooked.

The fact is that Bill is a gentleman of the Edwardian tradition, which partly explains why he is a host par excellence and, what is equally important, a perfect guest. In addition to his culinary accomplishments, he is an expert musician. And his innate charm makes him the beau of the town wherever he settles. There are few people of his sensibility and style around these days. These qualities are readily apparent throughout his book.

Bill is fortunate in having as his collaborator Helen Evans Brown, a superb cook and a veteran writer of cookbooks. Helen and I have kitchen-tested recipes together for months on end; we once covered most of the Great West in search of lore on wine, fish, cheese, and good food in general; and we have even circumnavigated the world together, sampling many an exotic dish along the way. Helen knows a good recipe when she sees it, and she was fascinated by the present collection. She has worked long and hard to put the recipes into standard culinary language, and she has tested all of them. When you set out to use this book you may be sure of having perfectly arranged recipes which work!

The recipes fit no cookbook pattern; they represent a personal collection — favorite dishes of Bill's and of his friends. Some come from his grandmother's old cook in Sacramento, some from various ladies of San Francisco, some from duchesses, and one or two from royalty. I have long said that good ingredients and simplicity are the important attributes of a good dish. That is precisely what you will find here — with a few festive overtones.

Let me commend this book to you. And in conclusion, I would like to quote, for the benefit of the authors, a line from the introduction to a favorite book of the 1890s, *Delicate Feasting*, by Mr. Theodore Child. The introduction was written by a Mr. P. Z. Didsbury.

"Adieu dear author[s]; *Macte virtute*, by which I mean continue in your efforts to win a glorious pair of gouty crutches, and believe me always your inseparable companion in Gastronomy."

JAMES A. BEARD

*New York City*

# Foreword

WHEN I THINK of the vast ocean of cookbooks already existent, I wonder at my temerity in pouring one more ounce of culinary water upon the present copious sea. My courage is revived by two thoughts.

I remember the countless times that I have been a host, and that my friends have been good enough to ask for my recipes, be it in France, in California, or in Italy. Thus I think my formulae are desirable ones.

Then again, I have always said that any cookbook is well worthwhile if it contains even *one* superlative dish. The price of the book is none too much for the possession of this outstanding recipe. How often have we not given a handsome tip to a chef or maître d'hôtel for some very coveted recipe, often, alas, to find that something had been left out? It is my wish that you will find *many* treasures in this collection, and that they will give you everlasting pleasure!

When one entertains, there are many things that are just as important as the presentation of perfectly cooked food: the welcome; the fastidiousness of the table with faultless linen, gleaming silver, shining glassware; the careful choosing of guests to make a harmonious whole, and their seating; the arrangement of flowers or fruit. Nothing must escape the eagle eye of the host. *No detail must be overlooked.*

[ xv ]

In the setting of the table, no matter how well trained the servant, a last look is very necessary to see that the flatware, china, and glasses are meticulously aligned, as though put there by measurements from a ruler — the "petit rien" to a well-thought-out ensemble. Even the chairs must be exactly placed!

The happy reception of guests is the opening strain of the evening's agreeable music. A warm, gracious greeting to each guest is better than any cocktail, and the pleasure of being so received often lasts for a very long time. Once I knew of a very famous French hostess who was noted for the warmth and cordiality she extended her guests. She went even further than that, finding time to go to the servants' dining hall to greet the chauffeurs, valets, and maids (yes, it was in *those* vanished days). She wished them *"Bon appétit"* and a pleasant time as long as they remained under her roof. This was the Princesse de Poix, grandmother of the present Duc de Mouchy, a lady with American blood in her veins. The Princesse is long since dead and gone, but her kindliness lives on to this day.

Brillat-Savarin says: "To entertain a guest is to charge one's self with that guest's comfort, and happiness, during all the time he is under one's roof." Also: "He who receives his friends *and has taken no personal interest in the preparation of the repast* is not worthy of having friends."

Such preparation takes time and thought. One main dish after another has to be considered, and when it has been decided upon, the rest of the meal is carefully built around it. REPEAT NOTHING! Don't have two starchy dishes, or two with cream in the component parts, or a pastry, such as a quiche Lorraine, at the start of a lunch and a lemon chiffon pie at its conclusion.

Also remember the words of the late Lady Mendl (Elsie de

[ xvi ]

Wolfe), a paragon of hostesses, author of a remarkable cookbook, in which she cautions: "Don't forget to have cold plates
cold, *cold,* COLD; and hot plates hot, *hot,* HOT!" It is quite
astonishing how frequently this advice is ignored. What is
worse than seeing a handsome, beautifully prepared hot dish,
served upon an ice-cold plate, congeal before your very eyes?
Or a crisp salad wilt upon a lukewarm one?

For those who entertain frequently, it is a good plan to have
a little book in which to record menus and guests invited for
the occasion. Then, when you are asking the Thistlethwaites
after a period of several months, you can consult your book
and not run the risk of repeating your former repast.

Menus on the table are useful. If you have a guest who is
finicky about his diet, he can then help himself more copiously
to one dish he prefers, and skip another. Also, most people
like to read a list of forthcoming fare.

Cookery is not a difficult art providing one looks upon it as
a delightful, *creative* adventure. But one must take the time
to do what is to be done, and to do it *leisurely.* DON'T RUSH!
And no shortcuts, either! If you are to serve a cold dessert at
dinner, prepare it in the morning, or even the night before.
Then it is off your mind. Pick over the salad greens, wrap them
in a cloth, and put in the refrigerator. They will need only the
dressing, which make and then set *that* aside. Thus two of
your principal courses are finished and out of the way. By plan-
ning and timing everything, all can be done in an easy sys-
tematic way. There need be no hustle or bustle, no hurry or
flurry. Then, when the first guests arrive, even though they
may be early, you are ready to greet them, calm as the oft-
mentioned cucumber.

In conclusion, one more wise word from Brillat-Savarin, who
usually manages to get himself mentioned in cookbooks: "*La*

*table est le seul endroit où l'on s'ennuie jamais pendant la première heure . . . Le plaisir de la table est de tous les âges, de toutes les conditions, de tous les pays, et de tous les jours. Il peut s'associer à tous les plaisirs et reste le dernier pour nous consoler de leur parte."*

WILLIAM TEMPLETON VEACH

*Les Muses*
*Bonnétable (Sarthe)*
*France*

# Contents

★

# Contents

# HORS D'OEUVRE
## and
# APPETIZERS

HORS D'OEUVRE
and
APPETIZERS

★
## Hors d'Oeuvre

These are a charming way of starting off any lunch, especially a Sunday one on the terrace or in the patio, where the
greater the variety the prettier the outlay. Of course, each
ravier (hors d'oeuvre dish) must be meticulously arranged and
garnished to make a lovely picture.

(1) *Eggs.* Cut hard-boiled eggs in halves. Remove yolks
and pass through a sieve; mix with mayonnaise, salt, paprika,
minced parsley, and minced chives. Fill whites.

(2) *Beans.* Dress very young cooked green beans with sauce
vinaigrette.

(3) *Carrots, Potatoes and Peas.* Mix diced cooked carrots,
diced cooked potatoes, and cooked peas with mayonnaise.

(4) *Potatoes.* Slice cold boiled potatoes thin, dress with salt
and pepper, olive oil and vinegar. Sprinkle with minced parsley.

(5) *Anchovies.* Make a purée of canned tuna by passing it
through a sieve, and season with lemon juice. Spread on fillets
of anchovies; roll up. Arrange on a dish and sprinkle with
chopped egg yolk and egg white, kept separate, and with
capers.

(6) *Artichokes à la Grecque.* Select 12 baby artichokes, remove outer leaves, and cut off top and stem. Combine in a
saucepan 1 cup of water, 2 tablespoons of olive oil, the juice
of a lemon, a pinch of salt, a dozen coriander seeds, and an
herb bouquet of parsley, bay, thyme, celery leaves, and fennel.

[ 3 ]

(If fennel isn't available, add a few fennel seeds.) Simmer for 5 minutes, then add the artichokes and cook until tender — about 20 minutes. Drain, dress with a little olive oil, and serve cold.

(7) *Artichoke Bottoms.* Fill cooked or canned artichoke bottoms with well-seasoned cooked peas, and glaze with aspic. (*Aspic:* Soften an envelope of gelatine in ⅛ cup of cold water, dissolve in a can of boiling consommé, season with Madeira and lemon juice, and cool to the consistency of unbeaten egg white. Spoon over artichokes and allow to set.)

(8) *Beets.* Slice cold cooked beets and dress with a sauce composed of 1 part of strong Dijon mustard to 2 parts of cream.

(9) *Mushrooms.* Slice raw mushrooms thin and marinate in French dressing for a couple of hours. Serve sprinkled with minced parsley.

(10) *Shrimp.* Mix small cooked shrimp with minced celery; dress with olive oil, vinegar, salt and pepper, and strew minced chives over the top.

(11) *Fennel.* Cut in thin slices, chill, and serve on chopped ice.

(12) *Ham and Melon.* Remove rind from a good ripe melon, slice, and serve with paper-thin slices of prosciutto (Italian ham).

(13) *Melon.* Cut in slices and serve with halved limes.

(14) *Radishes.* Select very tiny young ones, leave on a bit of the stems, and serve the French way — with fresh, unsalted butter.

(15) *Tuna.* Open a tin of Italian tuna packed in olive oil; turn out on a ravier; garnish with capers, parsley, and lemon wedges.

(16) *Onions à la Grecque.* Cook small peeled onions in the

same liquid as for artichokes à la Grecque (No. 6) until barely tender.

(17) *Sardines.* Arrange on a dish. Squeeze a little lemon juice over them, and garnish with lemon slices sprinkled with minced parsley.

(18) *Mussels Ravigote.* Discard all broken or open mussels. Scrupulously wash and brush the shells. Put in a deep pot with a cup of water and cook until they open. Cool, remove from shells, and mix with mayonnaise or ravigote dressing.

(19) *Salami.* A good Italian salami sliced thin, *thin,* THIN!

(20) *Tomatoes.* Slice thin and dress with French dressing and a sprinkle of parsley. I like tomatoes peeled, but the French rarely do.

(21) *Sweet Red Peppers.* Cut peppers in halves, discard stems and insides. Put in a large skillet with a tablespoon each of olive oil and water. Cover and cook slowly until the peppers are softened and the skins peel off easily. Cut in long strips, arrange in a dish, and dress with salt and pepper, the juices, and a little more olive oil, if necessary. *Very* good, and colorful.

(22) *Ratatouille.* (See pages 157-158.)

★
## Lobster Hors d'Oeuvre

This recipe is from Mrs. Cabot Brown.

Choose small lobsters and cook them in court bouillon (see Glossary) until they turn red — 15 or 20 minutes. Cool in the bouillon, then split down the center, remove flesh, and cut in bite-sized pieces. Put a toothpick in each piece and put back carefully in the cleaned shells. Arrange on a platter, decorate with crisp parsley, and have a bowl of good mayonnaise in which to dunk.

★
## *Beignets de Fromage*

¼ pound butter
1 cup boiling water
1 cup flour
1 teaspoon salt
4 eggs
Cayenne
1½ cups grated Parmesan cheese
2 tablespoons cornstarch
Deep fat for frying

Add butter to water and put over heat. As soon as the butter is melted, add flour and salt and stir vigorously until a ball forms. Remove from fire and add eggs, one at a time, and a dash of cayenne. Return to low fire and stir until the mixture leaves the sides of the pan. Add cheese and cornstarch, blend well, and cool for 3 hours. Drop by teaspoons into deep fat (375°) until puffed and golden. Drain on paper toweling and serve on a napkin, and at once!

★
## *Canapés Marquesa Esther Maurigi*

The Marquesa Maurigi has delightful cocktail parties, and she is one of the few people I know in the whole world to give a *large* one that is a pleasure to attend. To begin with, her Florentine villa is huge, so guests can circulate freely in the immense salons and be free from jostling, and the foolish chatter that usually accompanies such gatherings is lost in the noble spaces of the rooms. As this is the Marquesa's favorite form of convoking friends, she is ever on the search for new canapés and gewgaws for her parties, and she has a bewildering array of tempting morsels to beguile her friends. Knowing this penchant of the charming lady, I invented a canapé and named it for her.

Peel firm tiny egg or cherry tomatoes of uniform size, cutting a very thin slice from either end of each one, so that once it is cut in two you will have two minute cups. *Great care* must be taken in the peeling, slicing and cutting, for your object is to have from each tomato two tiny *nonleakable* cups. Scoop out the halves. Make a tomato aspic and, with a teaspoon, carefully fill each little tomato cup ¾ full with the liquid. Arrange the baby cups in a flat dish and put in the refrigerator to set. Just before serving, put in each tomato a bit of sieved hard-boiled egg — white and yolk — and add a dab of mayonnaise through a pastry tube to finish. In summer, serve in a dish set in cracked ice. Decorate with parsley.

★

## Codfish Balls

At the American Embassy in Rome, once upon a time, the Princesse Aymon de Faucigny-Lucinge, having never before tasted these delicacies, commandeered a small platter of them, vowing to eat nothing else. She kept her word!

1 pound boneless salt codfish
2 large baked potatoes
3 tablespoons butter
1 egg
2 to 4 tablespoons cream
Pepper
Deep fat for frying

Cover fish with cold water, bring just to a boil, then drain. Repeat twice. Pound in a mortar with a pestle or put in a heavy cloth and pound with a mallet. Remove potatoes from shells and mash smooth. You should have 2 cupfuls. Combine with the fish; add butter, and the egg beaten in 2 tablespoons of cream. Mix well, adding more cream if too stiff. Cool and form in tiny balls. Fry in deep fat at 370° until brown. Serve hot on toothpicks. Makes about 12 dozen.

★

## Anchovy Eggs

We go on inventing new things for cocktail parties, and they are good, bad, and indifferent. I think perhaps one of the most acceptable of these tidbits may be the grandfather of them all. Slice hard-boiled eggs; cut sliced bread in rounds slightly larger. Butter and spread with mayonnaise, then put a slice of egg on each. Top with a rolled anchovy, its middle decorated with a caper.

★

## Pistachio Stuffed Eggs

If you can find the smallest eggs, buy them for stuffing; one makes a much more agreeable mouthful than a larger egg. Cut hard-boiled eggs in two and cut a tiny slice from the bottom so each half will stand straight. Remove yolks and sieve. Mix with mayonnaise and finely ground pistachio nuts to your taste. Season with salt and pepper, fill whites, and decorate each egg with a leaf of parsley.

★

## Hot Biscuits with Foie Gras

This is one of the "spécialités" of my house. Cut biscuit dough with a very small cutter. When the biscuits come from the oven, quickly split, butter, and stuff with a small dab of foie gras. Mousse de foie gras can be used, but it's not quite

[ 8 ]

the same. Serve in an English muffin dish so the biscuits will stay hot. These disappear with fantastic rapidity.

★
## Pâté de Campagne Gascon

2 pounds pork liver
2 pounds fresh pork fat
3 egg yolks
1 tablespoon cornstarch
2 minced échalotes
1 clove garlic, puréed
2 tablespoons salt
1 teaspoon white pepper
½ teaspoon nutmeg
¼ teaspoon cloves
½ teaspoon ginger
¼ cup brandy
1 pound thinly sliced fresh
    pork fat (from back)

Pass the liver and fat through the finest blade of the meat grinder — a messy but efficacious procedure. Add other ingredients except sliced fat and mix very well. Line a 2-quart terrine with the pork fat slices, add the mixture, cover with more sliced pork fat, put in a bain-marie, and bake in a 350° oven for 2 hours or until the melted fat shows no color. Cool, preferably weighted down, and serve sliced on the cold meat platter or with a green salad. Also fine as an appetizer.

★
## Pâté of Livers

¼ pound calf liver
¼ pound chicken livers
½ cup Madeira

¾ pound fresh pork fat
3 eggs
¼ teaspoon nutmeg
3 minced échalotes
2½ teaspoons salt
1 tablespoon minced parsley
1 pound sliced pork fat (from back)

Marinate the livers in the Madeira overnight, turning a few times. Dry and grind, using the finest blade; grind fat also. Combine with eggs, herbs, and seasonings. Line a 1½-quart terrine with the thinly sliced pork fat, pour in mixture, cover with more pork fat, and cook in a bain-marie in a 350° oven for 2 hours or until the fat runs clear.

★

## Terrine of Chicken Liver

This recipe comes from the Hôtel du Chalet, Lamorlaye, whence very rare things emanate, for it was there that I got my poodle, Erica, from the wonderful kennels of the Princesse de Broglie, who is producing the best of this breed in Europe.

10 chicken livers
1 pound pork liver
2 medium onions
2 cloves garlic
10 ounces mousse of foie gras
1½ teaspoons salt
¼ teaspoon each pepper and nutmeg
1 pinch cloves
⅓ cup flour
5 eggs
1 jigger Cognac
1 jigger port
Thin slices pork fat

[ 10 ]

Pass livers, onions and garlic through a food chopper. Add foie gras, seasonings, flour, eggs, Cognac and port. Line a 3-cup terrine with the pork fat, pour in the mixture, cover with more sliced fat, and let stand in the refrigerator for 24 hours. Cover, put in a bain-marie, and bake in a 300° oven for 2 hours or until the melted fat is clear and shows no sign of pink. Serve cold with salad, in sandwiches, or for canapés.

★

## *Pissaladière*

Perhaps the most appreciated accompaniment I ever ate with a cocktail. I had gone one morning, in Vence, to inspect a house that was to be rented. I went alone and had a good peek through the various windows, so interested in my project that I never noticed the lowering clouds. Then the heavens opened. It was lunchtime and there I was, a long distance from town, the rain pelting down. Although I had heard that the people living next door to the empty house were disagreeable and not much liked by the majority of Vençeans, I decided to risk everything, including a rebuff, to ask if I might use their telephone. I reached the front door of the inviting villa looking like a drenched rat. A pleasant maid opened the door and said politely that I might telephone. And indeed, it was she who called the taxi. In the meantime, the "disagreeable" owner of the house came to where I was standing in the hallway. He kindly asked me to come and have a cocktail, as they were just having their pre-lunch drink. Nothing loath, I joined them, and not only did I have a very acceptable, warming martini, but the butler brought a dish containing something straight from heaven. It was the pissaladière, but such a glorified version! This is its duplicate:

Bake a shallow 8-inch pie crust, preferably of puff paste.

It must be very flaky. Sauté 6 large sliced onions in 2 table-spoons each of butter and olive oil until golden. Spread on the baked crust, arrange anchovy fillets over them in a crisscross or spoke pattern, and fill in spaces with black olives. Put in a 400° oven for 10 minutes or until piping hot, cut in wedges, and serve.

★

## Prosciutto with Italian Bread Sticks

Wrap Italian bread sticks (grissini) with paper-thin slices of prosciutto (Italian ham) or Parma ham. Seal with a bit of soft butter.

★

## Sardines and Cheese

This recipe came from the late Major Joseph Tilden, a very distinguished epicure and one of the brilliant members of the famous Bohemian Club.

Drain sardines, lay each on a finger of buttered bread, cover thickly with grated Parmesan cheese, and bake in a 350° oven until nicely browned. Sprinkle with minced parsley and a drop or two of lemon juice. Serve very hot.

★

## Sardine Appetizers

From Prince's Club, Colombo.

Use rather small sardines — the Norwegian brisling packed in oil is good; French sardines had better have bones removed and tails cut off. Make fingers of bread a little larger than French sardines or, if using brislings, large enough for about three. Butter the bread copiously. Lay the fish on the fingers; on each sardine put a pea of butter, a dash of cayenne, and a squeeze of lemon. Put in the oven long enough to toast the bread. You should be able to taste the cayenne.

★

## Toast with Ham

Run some baked Virginia or other well-flavored ham through the fine blade of the meat grinder. Season highly with mustard, salt and cayenne, add enough butter to make the mix spreadable, and serve on *hot* buttered toast.

SOUPS

★
## Bean Soup Tuscany Style

This is the way the soup is served at Nino's, in Rome.

Boil white beans (fagioli Romana), fresh if possible, with an onion until well cooked and soft, but not broken. In the bottom of a tureen put about ½ cup of olive oil, a heaping tablespoon of minced parsley and half that of minced basil, salt and a little pepper to taste, and plenty of finely chopped garlic. Over this place the beans; cover with good meat stock. Stir gently and serve piping hot. Serves six.

★ NOTE: *For the amount of seasoning above, you will need 2 or 3 cups of cooked beans and a quart of stock.* H.E.B.

★
## Cashew Nut Soup

This is a Ceylonese delicacy.

Make a roux of 2 tablespoons of butter and 1 tablespoon of flour; when well blended, add a quart of chicken broth and a pint of cream. Stir and mix well together, then add 2 cups of ground *raw* cashew nuts. Season with salt, pepper, and a little nutmeg. I cook this soup in a double boiler and let it cook until rich and velvety. It is both delicate and delicious. Serves six generously.

[ 17 ]

★

## Celery Root Soup

Phyllis Cahill went away one day forgetting to turn off the low flame under her soup pot. It contained a shredded celery root, an onion and a quart of water. When she returned, everything had simmered to a pulp; she added more water (a tin of consommé is even better), salt and pepper, and we sat down to a scrumptious soup.

★

## Crab Bisque

This is one of Mrs. Cutter's famous recipes. (See page 64.)

1 tablespoon butter
2 tablespoons flour
1 quart milk
1 quart cream
2 pounds picked crab meat
Salt and pepper

Make a roux with the butter and flour in upper part of a double boiler, add milk and cream, and cook until thickened and smooth. Fifteen minutes before serving, add the crab meat; this will give it time enough to flavor the soup but not to disintegrate. Season to taste with salt and pepper. Serves eight.

★

## Consommé Madrilène

3-pound shin of beef (bone and meat)
1 veal knuckle or calf's foot
3 large ripe tomatoes, or a No. 2 tin
An herb bouquet

[ 18 ]

1 sliced onion
1½ tablespoons salt
¼ teaspoon pepper, or a dash of cayenne
3 quarts cold water
3 egg whites

Put beef, veal, tomatoes, herbs, onion, seasonings, and water in a large pot, bring to a boil, and skim. Turn heat low and simmer for 4 hours, skimming occasionally. Turn heat up to reduce to 2 quarts; strain and cool. Refrigerate overnight and remove hard fat from top. Return to heat, add the egg whites, very slightly beaten, and bring to a boil, stirring constantly. Turn off heat and allow to settle, then strain through a wet cloth. Add a few drops of red coloring if necessary, and return to the refrigerator to jell. Serves eight.

★

## *Cream of Curry Soup*

2 tablespoons curry powder
1 quart chicken broth
4 egg yolks
1 cup thick cream
Salt and pepper
Powdered parsley

Mix curry powder in a cup with a little chicken broth (cold) and add it to the broth itself. Let heat for 10 minutes. In a bowl, mix the egg yolks with the cream. Salt and pepper the broth, add the egg-cream mixture, and stir until the boiling point is reached. Remove at once from the flame and set aside to cool. Serve thoroughly cold, in cups, with a slight sprinkle of powdered parsley. Serves six.

[ 19 ]

★
## Potage Crécy

Slice thin a pound of very nice young carrots and cook in ¼ cup of butter with 2 tablespoons of minced onion, salt and pepper, and a pinch of sugar. When cooked, add a quart of consommé and a cup of rice. Cover and cook gently over a low flame. When the rice is thoroughly cooked, pass all through a sieve, adding more consommé to thin. Also add a cup of cream. Reheat, adding a little more butter, and serve with small fried croûtons. Serves six.

★
## Potage Duchesse

2 cups chicken stock or bouillon
1 cup mashed potatoes
3 egg yolks
1 cup cream
¼ cup cooked chopped sorrel
Salt and pepper

Bring stock to a boil, remove from heat, add potatoes and mix until smooth. Beat egg yolks with cream and whip into soup, then add sorrel, and salt and pepper to taste. Return to low heat and stir constantly until well heated. If necessary, add more seasoning and more stock or cream to thin. Serve very hot to four.

★ NOTE: *This soup is also delicious cold.* H.E.B.

★
## Potage Marie-Louise

3 leeks
3 turnips
3 potatoes

2 slices bread
1½ quarts bouillon or beef stock
2 cups milk
2 egg yolks
Salt and pepper

Peel and slice vegetables, cut crusts from bread and put all in a large pot. Add bouillon and simmer 4 hours, then force through a sieve. Mix milk and egg yolks, and add to soup. Heat gently, correcting seasoning. This soup should not be too thick. Serves six.

★

## French Onion Soup

This recipe comes from my great friend Alice Requa Low, who, as wife of Admiral Francis Low, was a distinguished hostess on the West Coast.

6 medium onions, sliced thin
3 tablespoons butter
2 tablespoons flour
6 cups consommé
Salt and pepper
6 slices toasted French bread
Grated Parmesan cheese

Cook onions in butter until soft but not brown. Sprinkle in flour and stir several minutes, then add consommé, and salt and pepper to taste. Put toast in an earthenware tureen and sprinkle generously with cheese. Pour the soup over it, sprinkle another handful of cheese over the top, and put in the oven long enough to brown. Serves six. This may, of course, be made in individual onion-soup pots.

★
## *Potage Maison*

This is a soup I often serve at my own dinner parties.

½ pound lean beef
½ pound lean veal
1 veal shin bone
1 pound beef bones, cut in pieces
1 small chicken
3 tomatoes
3 turnips
3 beets
3 carrots
3 leeks
1 or 2 onions
10 peppercorns
3 ribs celery with leaves
½ cup parsley
1 tablespoon salt
3 egg whites

Put all ingredients except egg whites in a large pot and completely cover with cold water. Bring to a boil, skim, cover, turn heat low, and simmer 5 hours. Strain, cool, remove fat and clarify as in Consommé Madrilène. Serve with tiny fried croûtons. Serves six or eight.

For *borscht*, I add some grated raw beets and simmer 15 minutes before serving with sour cream.

★
## *Tomato Chicken Consommé*

This soup's greatest asset is its color.

1 small chicken, cut up
2 pounds ripe tomatoes, cut up

2 quarts chicken broth (made from backs and necks)
An herb bouquet
Salt and pepper
1 egg white

Put chicken, tomatoes, broth, herb bouquet, and 2 teaspoons of salt in a large pot and bring to a boil. Reduce heat, skim, and simmer until the liquid is reduced to 6 cups. Strain, correct seasoning, and proceed as in Consommé Madrilène. Serves six. This may be served hot, with some of the chicken breast cut up in it as a garnish, or iced.

★

## Yellow Tomato Soup

Make a madrilène, using *yellow* egg tomatoes instead of red. Tincture before serving with a little *yellow* food color, for the real reason for this soup is its *yellowness*. Also add a definite dash of powdered ginger to "relever" the taste. Serve chilled with a yellow nasturtium on top of each cup.

★ NOTE: *Yellow tomatoes are a* MUST *for this soup, but I daresay it could be served without the nasturtium, pretty as that might be.* H.E.B.

★

## Jellied Tomato Bouillon

6 large ripe tomatoes or 1 No. 2½ can tomatoes
1½ cups water
Celery leaves or ½ teaspoon celery salt
½ bay leaf
2 cloves
2 teaspoons salt
2 envelopes plain gelatine
2 teaspoons lemon juice

[ 23 ]

Dash of Tabasco
1 small onion, minced
Minced parsley
Minced chives

Simmer tomatoes, 1 cup of water, seasonings, and onion for 25 minutes. Strain, pressing out all liquid. Return to heat and add gelatine that has been softened in ½ cup of cold water. Stir until dissolved. Correct seasoning and chill. Serve in cups and garnish with minced parsley and chives. Serves six.

★ NOTE: *A spoonful of sour cream on each serving is a nice touch.* H.E.B.

★

## Tourin

In Gascony, where this excellent soup was born, it is known as "soupe des ivrognes," as it is said to be an excellent antidote for a hangover. I am very partial to this soup, although not for that reason, as happily nature and prudence have combined to save me from those unfortunate rebellions of the human system!

Cook 2 good-sized sliced onions in 2 tablespoons of butter and 2 tablespoons of olive oil until wilted and beginning to take color. Then cover with a quart of water, lower the flame, and let simmer, covered, about 2 hours. Put 3 egg yolks in a bowl, along with 4½ teaspoons of wine vinegar, and beat together. Pour the steaming onions over this and serve, having a thin slice of crusty French bread in each soup plate. This soup can be enhanced by adding a clove or two or three of garlic, sliced, and indeed, it is very good with even more! That is, if you like garlic, as I happen to. Serves two.

FISH
and
SHELLFISH

★

## *Brandade of Codfish*

If you like garlic, you will find this a wonderful dish.

> 1 pound salt codfish
> 1½ cups warm olive oil
> 1½ cups warm cream
> 2 cloves garlic, puréed
> Lemon juice and (optional) grated rind
> Salt and pepper

It is advisable to buy fish in prepared fillets, skinned and more or less boned. Prepare fish by putting it into a saucepan of cold water and letting it come *just to the boil,* then whisk off the flame, pour off water, and fill with cold water. Repeat this process and then taste, as some fish is saltier than others. If the fish is still too salty, pour off water and repeat a third time. Remember never to let the water boil, for that will toughen the fish. Now push the pan to the back of the stove, or reduce the heat, and poach for 10 minutes. Then lift fish out, drain thoroughly, and flake. Put fish in a small wooden bowl or mortar and pound it to smithereens with a wooden potato masher or pestle. Transfer pounded fish to a double boiler to keep it warm, and begin as you would with mayonnaise, dropping in a little olive oil and then a little warm cream alternately, stirring all the time, until the mixture is an unctuous paste. Add garlic, a little lemon juice, and (optional)

[ 27 ]

a little grated lemon rind, pepper freshly ground from the mill and, if need be, a suspicion of salt. Always keep the dish warm in the making. If left to stand, the oil sometimes has a tendency to separate.

Sometimes chopped truffles are added, but in my opinion that is a bit pretentious, as the dish is primarily a simple peasant one. I like to serve brandade with a purée of potatoes, but some like plain boiled spuds. In Nîmes, France, they stir the brandade into the puréed potatoes.

★ NOTE: *This can be made in an electric blender, in which case fish, oil, and cream should all be hot.* H.E.B.

★

## Crab Legs in Buttery, Winey Sauce

One of the best recipes in this book. You must wheedle or browbeat your fishmonger to sell you the crab legs, counting upon about 10 per person. In San Francisco, where the Dungeness crabs are superlative, these crustaceans have large juicy legs, and that is what you need.

Put ½ pound of butter in a saucepan with ¾ to 1 cup of good dry white wine, some tarragon, a small sprig of rosemary, a little thyme, and some parsley. Let this simmer slowly to reduce by half, then set aside to cool somewhat. Now dip each crab leg into the sauce, and then roll in fine cracker crumbs, salting and peppering lightly. Arrange on a flat baking dish, sprinkling a little sauce over, and gild under the broiler, turning to brown a bit on the other side. Pile on a platter. Pass the rest of the sauce through a sieve, and pour it over the crab legs just before serving. This sauce suffices for 60 legs.

In case it is not possible to obtain so many legs, false ones may be devised by mixing chopped crab meat with a thick Béchamel, forming teaspoons of the mixture into the shape of legs. Then, when these croquettes are good and cold, proceed as above. The taste will be the same.

★

## Lobster Croquettes with Olympia Oyster Sauce

1 pound (2 cups) lobster meat
1 cup thick Béchamel sauce
1 teaspoon minced parsley
1 teaspoon lemon juice
Salt and pepper
1 beaten egg
Flour
Cracker crumbs
Deep fat

Mix lobster, sauce, parsley and lemon juice, and salt and pepper, to taste. Chill, then shape into 12 croquettes, roll in flour, dip in egg, then roll in cracker crumbs. Let stand to dry, then fry in deep fat at 375°. Drain on paper toweling. Put in center of platter and surround with oyster sauce (below). Serves six.

★

## Olympia Oyster Sauce

1 cup sauce Mornay
100 Olympia oysters

Combine sauce Mornay with oysters and juice. Heat gently.
★ NOTE: *This is probably about 1 cup of oysters, as they are minuscule.* H.E.B.

★

## Lobster and Shrimp in Curry Sauce

1 2-pound lobster
1 tablespoon salt

1 sliced onion
1 crushed clove garlic
2 sliced carrots
24 green jumbo shrimp or prawns

Put lobster in cold water to cover. Add other ingredients except shrimp, and bring to a boil. Simmer 15 minutes. Add shrimp, cook 5 minutes, then cool the shellfish in the broth. Shell, and return shells to broth to use in making the sauce. Slice lobster; clean shrimp, and cut each in halves. Reheat in curry sauce (below).

Serve with pilaf and the following:

2 dozen popadums, cooked according to directions on tin.
Bombay duck, crisped in the oven, then shredded.
Finely minced onion.
Hard-boiled eggs, whites and yolks sieved separately.
Several kinds of chutney — hot and sweet.
Chopped peanuts.
Crisply fried crumbled bacon.
Small unpeeled bananas, one per person (these are to cool the mouth if need be).
Quartered limes.
Bhurta. To make: grind 6 red peppers, then squeeze through a cloth, extracting all juices. Add enough cayenne to the pulp to make it frightfully hot. Form in a little ball, and warn your guests that a little goes a long way.

★

## Curry Sauce

2 large sliced onions
2 sliced cloves garlic

¼ pound butter ( 1 bar )
1 peeled and sliced apple
1 peeled and sliced eggplant
2 tablespoons curry powder
Salt and pepper
1 cup grated coconut
½ teaspoon sugar
1 cup cream

Cook onions and garlic in butter until soft. Add apple and eggplant, and when they begin to take color, add the curry powder (more, if you like it hot) and salt and pepper to taste. Add coconut and ½ cup of the strained hot court bouillon in which the shellfish cooked. Simmer ½ hour, then add 2 cups more bouillon and cook another hour and a half. Force through a sieve, add sugar, correct seasoning. Stir in cream just before serving. Serves eight.

★

## Cold Lobster Soufflé

This recipe comes from the cookbook of Mrs. Audrey Emery, and I have it from her niece, Mrs. George Post, Jr.

2 medium-sized cooked lobsters
1½ cups good mayonnaise
Salt and pepper
2 envelopes plain gelatine
2 cups consommé
½ cup cream, whipped

Cut lobster meat into small pieces, mix with mayonnaise, and season to taste. Soften gelatine in cold consommé and melt over hot water. Cool and add half of it to lobster. Pour remainder in a shallow pan and allow to set to an aspic in the refrigerator. Add whipped cream to the lobster, pour in a soufflé dish and chill. Decorate with aspic, chopped, and any coral the lobster might have had. Serves six.

★

## Escalloped Oysters

This is from my grandmother's cookbook.

Mix 3 cups of dry bread crumbs (or cracker crumbs) with a cup of melted butter. Put a layer in the bottom of a baking dish, add a layer of oysters, salt and pepper, and repeat until you've used a quart of oysters. The top layer should be crumbs. Pour a cup of white wine over all and bake for 20 minutes in a 450° oven. Serves six to eight.

★

## Fried Oysters

These are delicious. The recipe comes from the famous old Delmonico's in New York, which our parents and grandparents used to love.

Dry Eastern oysters by wrapping in a cloth. Season with salt and pepper. Dip in lightly beaten egg, then roll in fine cracker crumbs. Have equal parts of lard and butter in a skillet, boiling hot. Drop in your oysters, and when gilded on both sides, drain on paper, squeezing a little lemon juice over. Serve en dôme, garnished with quartered lemons. Fried parsley can well accompany the oysters.

★

## Portland Oyster Custard

1 pint cream
1 pint oysters
5 eggs, beaten slightly
Salt and pepper

[ 32 ]

Mix together and pour into a buttered baking dish. Bake in a bain-marie in a 350° oven until set. Serve with either sauce Mornay or hollandaise. Or bake the custard in a ring mold, and serve with the center filled with crab masked with one of those sauces. Or fill small buttered darioles with the mixture, bake, unmold, and pour hollandaise over them. For this last suggestion, use tiny Olympia oysters in the custard.

★
## Salmon Cutlets
This is James A. Beard's recipe.

Remove fish from a 1-pound tin of red salmon; drain thoroughly and pick out the bones and skin. Mix the fish with 2 cups of mashed potatoes, 1 tablespoon of grated onion, 1½ teaspoons of salt, and 1 teaspoon of paprika. Blend well. Then shape into cutlets, roll in flour, dip in beaten egg, and lastly roll in fine cracker crumbs. Chill an hour. Put in basket and fry in deep hot fat, heated to 390°. Serve with egg sauce or hollandaise.

★
## Egg Sauce
⅓ cup butter
3 tablespoons flour
½ teaspoon salt
⅛ teaspoon pepper
1½ cups hot water or cream
2 hard-boiled eggs
1 teaspoon lemon juice

Melt half the butter in a double boiler; add flour, salt and pepper, and stir until smooth. Add hot water or cream and cook 5 minutes, stirring all the while. Then add 2 hard-boiled eggs, well chopped. Add lemon juice and remaining butter at the last moment. If you have used cream, take care that the sauce does not curdle.

★

## Kippered Salmon

This is also from Mrs. Audrey Emery's private cookbook; it is included for those fortunate ones who have a whole salmon.

Take a 12-pound salmon, a nice fat specimen, and after cleaning, split it down the back. Then, two or three times a day, rub into it the following:

1 cup dark brown sugar, tightly packed
2 tablespoons black pepper
2 tablespoons coarse salt

Let the fish lie in the liquid which forms, turning it over, preferably skin side down at night. Marinate thus for two or three days. Cut in steaks 2 inches thick. Wrap in well-buttered paper and fry in butter until brown. Serve hot in the papillotes.

★

## Fried Sardines

From Château de Bonnétable, Sarthe, France.

Choose the finest large boneless Portuguese or French sardines, packed in olive oil. Drain, roll in flour, and carefully place in a frying basket. Drop into hot (380°) deep fat, and lift out again at once. Serve with fried parsley. Allow 2 or 3 sardines for each person.

★
## Sole Caprice

Dredge 12 small fillets of sole in flour, dip in beaten egg, and roll in fine crumbs. Peel 6 small bananas, cut in halves, and dust with flour. Put them in a well-buttered pan, spread each with soft butter, and put in a 350° oven until lightly browned. Sauté the fillets in butter, arrange on a platter, and top with the bananas, lifting them carefully with a spatula. Cover with hollandaise sauce, then sprinkle with minced parsley. Serves six.

★
## Sole Papillote

This is truly epicurean.

> 6 small fillets of sole
> Milk
> Melted butter
> 24 shelled crab legs
> Salt and pepper
> ¼ pound sautéed sliced mushrooms
> 4 slices crisp bacon
> 6 sheets good bond typewriter paper

Soak fish in milk to cover for several hours. Drain and wipe dry, and lay each fillet in the center of a sheet of paper, which has been generously buttered. Dip crab legs in butter and arrange 4 on top of each fillet; sprinkle with salt and pepper and divide the mushrooms and bacon (crumbled) among them. Top each with ½ teaspoon of butter, fold paper, and secure edges with a double fold. Bake in a 450° oven for 20 minutes. Serve in the paper, cutting the top with sharp-pointed scissors. Serves six.

★

## Sole Duglère

Poach 12 small fillets of sole in court bouillon (see Glossary), taking care to cook only until they have lost their translucency. Arrange on a well-buttered baking dish in a straight row. Make a hollandaise sauce and to it add 2 tomatoes, peeled, seeded and cut in shreds, and 1 cup of sliced sautéed mushrooms. Cover the fish with this, sprinkle with grated Parmesan cheese, and brown quickly in the oven. Serves six.

★

## Fillets of Sole in Champagne

I got this recipe many years ago from a steward on the *Île de France*.

> 6 fillets of sole
> Salt and pepper
> 6 minced échalotes
> 2 tablespoons butter
> Champagne (or dry white wine)
> Hollandaise sauce
> 6 rondelles of cooked lobster (slices of tail meat)
> Truffles (optional)

Divide fillets in half lengthwise, sprinkle with salt and pepper, and either fold or roll. Tie with thread or fasten with picks to hold their form. Cook shallots in butter; when they are wilted, pour into the pan (which must not be of iron) enough champagne to poach the fillets. When the fish is done, which will take only a few minutes, put on an ovenproof platter and keep warm. Reduce poaching liquid to ½ cup and strain into hollandaise. Place a slice of lobster on each fillet, add a slice of truffle if you are lucky, and pour sauce quickly over all. Brown quickly in a 400° oven. Serves six.

# CHEESE
## and
# EGG DISHES

★

## Crème au Fromage

Butter
2 ounces (½ cup) grated Gruyère cheese
½ cup cream
6 eggs
½ teaspoon salt
Pepper
1 cup hollandaise sauce
2 tablespoons tomato paste

Butter 6 ramekins or darioles (or small custard cups) and powder them with grated cheese. Beat together the remaining cheese, cream, eggs, salt, and a grinding or two of pepper. Divide among the molds. Put the molds in a pan, fill with enough hot water to reach halfway up the molds, and bake for 25 to 40 minutes in a 350° oven, until a knife inserted in the center comes out clean. Turn out on a platter and cover with the hollandaise sauce to which the tomato paste has been added. Serves six.

★ NOTE: *This is delicious served on a bed of puréed spinach, surrounded with thin slices of Virginia ham. The sauce is known as Sauce Choron.* H.E.B.

★

## Fonduta Piemontese

To make this delicate dish from Italy, one must have a tin of white truffles, procurable in any of the fine specialty shops.

1 pound Fontina cheese (Italian cheese, from Aosta)
1 cup milk
2 tablespoons (¼ bar) butter
5 egg yolks
1 tin (1 or 2 ounces) white truffles, sliced thin
Buttered toast fingers

Cut the cheese in bits; soften in the milk in a double boiler. Add the butter and lightly beaten egg yolks after the cheese has entirely melted. Stir until creamy. Then add the truffles. Serve at once, putting the mixture in a chafing dish or one that fits over hot water. The fonduta must be kept hot. It is eaten with buttered fingers of toast, everyone dipping into the marvelous concoction. Serves four as a main course, eight or ten as an appetizer.

The white truffle has its own special perfume and is extraordinarily aromatic. It is perfectly delicious when taken in small doses. Too much in too short a time can sate the palate. The smell of the raw white truffle is so powerful that it is against the law in Italy to travel in a train with a parcel of them, for fear of asphyxiating fellow passengers!

★ NOTE: *This fonduta makes a superb appetizer. If buttered toast fingers seem too rich, try Italian breadsticks.* H.E.B.

★

### On Making Soufflés

There is nothing terrifying about making a soufflé. In fact, nothing is easier if one bears in mind certain precautions. Here are my rules:

(1) The thick Béchamel sauce which is the base of the soufflé must be cool; it can be made in advance.

(2) The other ingredients of the soufflé should be prepared

just before the cooking, especially the beaten egg whites, which are folded in last.

(3) The mold or soufflé dish should be well buttered.

(4) The oven should be preheated to a moderate heat (350°).

(5) When cooked, RUSH TO THE TABLE. Soufflés simply won't wait.

★

## Cheese Soufflé

2 tablespoons butter
3 tablespoons flour
½ cup scalded milk
½ cup (or a little more) grated cheese,
    half Parmesan, half Gruyère
¼ teaspoon salt
Dash of cayenne
3 eggs

Put butter in double boiler, add flour and blend well. Stir in milk. When smooth, add grated cheese, salt and cayenne. Stir until the cheese melts. Remove from fire and add 3 beaten egg yolks. Let the mixture cool, and then fold in the stiffly beaten egg whites. Pour into a buttered 3- or 4-cup soufflé dish and bake in a moderate oven (350°) for half an hour. Serves two or three.

★

## Florence's Cheese Soufflé

This is my sister's recipe.

3 tablespoons butter
3 tablespoons flour
¾ cup milk

½ teaspoon salt
Dash of cayenne
1 cup grated Tillamook cheese
3 eggs

In double boiler make white sauce with the butter, flour, milk and seasonings, cooking it for 10 minutes. Add the cheese and stir until melted. Then remove from the fire and add the beaten egg yolks. Let cool and fold in the stiffly beaten egg whites. Pour into a buttered 3- or 4-cup soufflé dish and bake in a moderate oven (350°) ½ hour. The Tillamook cheese, from Oregon, gives a flavor of its own, rather mild, and has a nice yellow color. Serves three or four.

★ NOTE: *If you can't find Tillamook cheese, any mild Cheddar will do, for that's what Tillamook is.* H.E.B.

★

## Eggs Mollet

Have the desired number of eggs at room temperature, and put in a deep frying basket. Fill the pan with water and bring to a boil, lower eggs into it, cover and remove from heat. Allow to stand for 8 minutes, then plunge into cold water and remove shells with the greatest care. If they are to be used for a hot dish, place them in a pan of warm water.

★

## Eggs Mollet, Purée of Mushrooms

Recipe from H.R.H. La Princesse Isabelle de Bourbon, Comtesse Roger de la Rochefoucauld.

Wash ½ pound of mushrooms, discard tough ends of stems, and chop very fine. Stew in 2 tablespoons of butter for 10 minutes, then sprinkle with a tablespoon of flour, season with salt and pepper, and blend well over heat. Add 1 cup of cream

[ 42 ]

and cook until smooth and thick. Put in the center of a platter and arrange 4 eggs mollet on top. Serve at once to four.

★ NOTE: *These may be served in individual dishes for a nice first course.* H.E.B.

★

## Eggs Mollet, Curry Sauce

This recipe is from Mrs. George Post, Jr. It is excellent for lunch.

Arrange the desired number of eggs mollet on a bed of fluffy white rice, and cover with curry sauce.

★

## On Poaching Eggs

Have a pan that can hold water at least 3 inches deep; the pan must be large enough to prevent the eggs from touching one another. Have on a plate 1 tablespoon of cold water. When water in the pan boils, pour in 1 tablespoon of vinegar. Carefully break eggs on the wet plate, and slide into simmering water. Poach for 3 minutes. Remove with a skimmer and trim.

These eggs, trimmed of any slight irregularity, are much more attractive, to my way of thinking, than when cooked in those little gadgets which give the egg a much too perfect form — just as a spoonful of potatoes or rice on a plate is much nicer to look at than the same scooped up with an ice cream scoop.

★

## On Boiling Eggs

Place eggs in a saucepan of cold water. Bring water slowly to the boiling point. If you want your eggs very soft, remove them as soon as the water reaches the boil. Otherwise, cover and simmer for 2 minutes for soft eggs; 3 to 5 minutes for medium-cooked eggs; 12 to 15 minutes for hard eggs. To peel hard-boiled eggs, let stand in cold water for several minutes; the cold will make the egg draw away from the inner shell.

★

## Scrambled Eggs

I find it easier to scramble eggs in a Pyrex double boiler than over direct heat, and the results are more satisfactory. Remove from the hot water when the eggs are still a little liquid, as they will go on cooking in their own heat. If, in spite of your vigil, the eggs are a little dry, add a couple of spoons of cream, or a small egg of butter, and stir into the eggs.

★

## Molded Eggs

Take small ramekins, round or oval, and butter them *well*. If you like, decorate the bottoms with truffle, or ham, or tarragon leaves.

Into each, carefully break an egg. Set the ramekins in a bain-marie and let simmer slowly on top of the stove for 3 to 4 minutes. Then put in a 350° oven for the same length of time. The whites will cook, but the yolks will remain runny. Now lift the ramekins out and let them stand a couple of minutes before running a knife with a very thin blade around the edges of the eggs. Turn them out on fried croûtons of bread, cut in a size to fit the eggs.

★

## Poached Eggs, Sauce Madère

A special dish at the French country house of Madame de Chazelles, one of my neighbors in the Sarthe. Madame de

[ 44 ]

Chazelles is very gay and kindly, and much loved by the entire countryside as well as by the villagers. To lunch or dine with her is a gastronomic gala, and the meal is punctuated by the presence of nine white cats, a pet rooster, and a most absurb duck, named Gédéon, who sits and quacks to himself in a mirror that has been put at the dining room door for his pleasure.

Lightly fry bread in butter; spread with a little mousse de foie gras. Place poached eggs on the toast, and mask with a good lively sauce Madère. Do the masking just long enough in advance for the toast to sop a very little in the sauce.

★

## Poached Eggs in a Cheese Soufflé

This intriguing dish comes from the Ritz in Paris, where it is called Eggs Odette. It serves eight.

> 4 tablespoons butter
> 4 tablespoons flour
> 1 teaspoon salt
> Dash of cayenne
> 2 cups scalded cream
> ½ cup grated cheese (Gruyère and Parmesan, mixed)
> 8 egg yolks, lightly beaten
> 8 egg whites, stiffly beaten
> 8 poached eggs or eggs mollet

Melt butter in double boiler; add flour, salt and pepper. Mix well and add scalded cream, stirring thoroughly. Add grated cheese and stir until melted. Remove from the fire and stir in the egg yolks. When blended, set aside to cool, then add the beaten whites of the eggs, folding in nicely.

For the success of this dish you should have a long earthenware dish, with sides 2 inches or more in height. Butter it and pour in half of the soufflé mixture. Then carefully arrange the poached eggs (or eggs mollet) on the mixture. Spoon over the eggs the rest of the soufflé mixture, and bake in the oven as you would any soufflé.

★

## Hot Stuffed Eggs

8 to 10 large mushrooms
2 tablespoons butter
12 hot hard-boiled eggs
1 tablespoon catsup
2 tablespoons grated Parmesan cheese
Hot cream
Salt and pepper
Hollandaise sauce

Mince mushrooms and cook in butter until tender. Peel eggs, cut in halves, and remove yolks. Cut off a little slice at the bottom of the whites so they will stand upright, and arrange on a buttered baking dish; cover and keep warm in a low oven (250°). Working quickly, mash the yolks, add catsup and cheese, and enough cream to make the proper consistency. Season to taste with salt and pepper. Fill egg whites, cover, and return to the oven until warmed through (a hot oven will toughen the eggs). Cover with hollandaise sauce before serving. Serves six.

★

## Stuffed Eggs in Cheese Sauce

Hard-boil 12 eggs, then cut in half lengthwise. Arrange the whites in pairs to facilitate getting the right halves together after the stuffing process. Pass the yolks through a sieve, adding enough melted butter to make a paste. Season with salt,

[ 46 ]

pepper, a bit of dry mustard, and a little finely minced parsley. Stuff the hollows with this mixture and put the whites
together. Arrange them on a flat buttered earthenware dish.
Pour the cheese sauce over, masking the eggs well. Sprinkle
a little grated Parmesan on top, and pop into the oven long
enough to gild slightly.

★

## Cheese Sauce

Melt 2 tablespoons of butter, add a tablespoon of cornstarch
blended with a little water and stir smooth. Add 2 cups of
rich milk or cream and cook, stirring, over low heat, until
thick and smooth. Add a cup of grated Parmesan and salt and
pepper to taste. Stir smooth and serve.

★

## Dutch Eggs

Generously butter as many darioles or custard cups as you
have guests. Sprinkle with grated Parmesan cheese, being sure
that some adheres to the sides. Pour into each a beaten egg,
sprinkle with salt, cover generously with more grated cheese,
and dot with butter. Put the molds in a bain-marie and bake
in a 350° oven for about 12 minutes. Turn out on a dish and
serve with tomato sauce.

★

## Scrambled Eggs Beaulieu

A lunch starter from Beaulieu, the famous Latour Vineyards
in Napa Valley, California. The owner, the Marquise de Pins,
has many exquisite recipes.

Peel and seed 2 pounds of ripe tomatoes; chop, and stew
gently until the liquid is absorbed. Season with salt and

pepper. Slice 4 green peppers and cook in 3 tablespoons of butter until softened but still bright green. Scramble 8 or 10 eggs and put in the center of a platter. Surround with a border of the tomatoes, then with a border of the peppers. This is as pretty to look at as it is good to eat.

★

## Scrambled Eggs in a Rice Ring

2 pounds ripe tomatoes
6 échalotes
2 tablespoons butter
1 teaspoon tarragon
1 tablespoon minced parsley
¼ teaspoon thyme
Salt, pepper, and sugar
Rice or rice pilaf
Scrambled eggs

Peel tomatoes, remove seeds and chop; chop échalotes. Add butter and herbs and simmer until the sauce is thick and rather dark in color. Season with salt and pepper to taste, and a pinch of sugar. Pack hot rice or rice pilaf in a ring mold, then turn out on a serving dish and fill center with scrambled eggs. Surround with the tomato sauce.

★

## Nelle Savoyarde

This excellent dish hails from Savoy, as its name indicates. Strangely enough, I have rarely seen it served in France.

½ pound thinly sliced cooked ham
2 tablespoons flour
2 tablespoons butter
2 cups rich milk or cream

¼ pound (1½ cups) grated Gruyère cheese
6 eggs
Salt and pepper

Line bottom and sides of a rather low charlotte mold (an 8- or 9-inch round pan about 2 inches deep is ideal) with the ham, having the slices overlap and hang slightly over the top. Make a roux with the flour and butter; add milk and cook, stirring, until smooth and thick. Add cheese, and then beat in eggs, one at a time. Season to taste with salt and pepper, and pour into the ham-lined mold. Put in a larger pan with water coming halfway up the mold, cover and simmer over very low heat for 1½ hours, then put in a 300° oven for 15 minutes. Let stand a few minutes, then turn out on a serving dish and serve with tomato sauce, sauce Madère, or sauce Mornay.

★ NOTE: *This can be baked in a 300° oven in a pan of hot water. It will be done when a knife, inserted near the center, comes out clean. H.E.B.*

★

# Egg and Onion Casserole (*Oeufs à la Tripe*)

This is an excellent lunch dish, and also most acceptable for supper after the theater, as it can be prepared in advance. When you return late, it is only necessary to light the oven and heat.

8 mild onions
8 hard-boiled eggs
Salt and pepper
2 cups sauce Mornay
2 tablespoons grated Parmesan cheese
¼ cup cracker crumbs
2 tablespoons butter

Peel and slice the onions and steam over hot water until tender. Peel and slice eggs. Arrange the eggs, the onions and the sauce in alternate layers in a shallow baking dish, sprinkling each layer with salt and pepper. Sprinkle the top with cheese and crumbs, dot with butter, and bake in a 350° oven until hot and brown. Serves six.

★

## Scrambled Eggs à l'Infante

1 pound (or more) tiny cooked shrimps
¾ cup (1½ bars) butter
1 large vol-au-vent case
20 eggs
Salt and pepper
1 truffle

Heat the shrimps in the butter, and heat the vol-au-vent in the oven. Butter a shallow earthenware baking dish very generously. Beat the eggs well, season with salt and pepper, and pour into dish. Put over very low heat and stir with a wooden spoon until creamy. When the eggs are *à point*, which in this case means a little runny, add the hot shrimps and butter, pour into the vol-au-vent case, and cover the top with truffle, sliced thin. Serves eight to ten.

★

## Custard for Darioles

Alfred Lunt is very enthusiastic about serving these little custards at a late supper, hot or cold, with appropriate sauce. He is quite right, as there is no danger of "dreaming of one's grandmother" after partaking thereof. (I never mind dreaming of my grandmother, who was a charming old lady.)

Butter
5 eggs
3 egg yolks
½ teaspoon salt
2 cups thin cream
Nutmeg
Grated Parmesan (optional)

Butter 8 dariole molds (or custard cups) generously. Beat eggs and egg yolks slightly; add salt. Heat cream and add to eggs, along with a little nutmeg. If desired, powder the inside of the molds with cheese. Divide mixture among molds. Put a paper towel in the bottom of a large pan, put darioles on it, and pour in hot water to come halfway up the molds. Cover with waxed paper and bake in a 350° oven for 45 minutes, or until a knife comes out clean. Unmold and serve with Mornay, mushroom or tomato sauce.

★

## Eggs Hollandaise

This comes from Château de Bonnétable, Sarthe, France.

Make individual pastry shells, just large enough to hold a poached egg or an egg mollet. Put a hot egg into each shell and top with hollandaise mousseline.

★ NOTE: *Bill Veach served this dish to my husband and me when we visited him in Bonnétable. The sauce is made by folding a cup of cream, whipped, into a cup of hollandaise.* H.E.B.

★

## Ham Soufflé

½ pound ham
¼ cup (½ bar) butter

¼ cup flour
1 cup milk
4 eggs, separated
Salt and pepper
Nutmeg

Pound the ham in a mortar, or grind very fine. Make a sauce with the butter, flour and milk. Add beaten egg yolks, ham, salt, pepper, and nutmeg to taste. Beat egg whites until stiff and fold into mixture. Turn into a buttered quart soufflé dish and bake in a bain-marie in a 350° oven for 20 to 25 minutes. Serves four.

★

## Eggs and Asparagus for Lunch

This is a good recipe for those watching their waistlines.

Boil about 16 nice spears of fine green asparagus. Salt the water and take great care not to overcook. Then drain and arrange on a baking platter in two piles, tips in the center, facing the one the other. Put a generous walnut of butter in the center and break 4 eggs over it. Sprinkle over the eggs some grated Parmesan, dot with a little more butter, and season with salt and pepper. Put in a 300° oven long enough for the eggs to set.

★ NOTE: *It might be even better for waistlines if the butter were skipped.* H.E.B.

MEATS (including innards)

★
## Beefsteak with Oyster Sauce

Order a fine thick juicy beefsteak, large enough for eight. Put 3 dozen oysters (or 1½ pints of Olympias) in their liquid on the stove. When the boiling point is reached, skim and remove oysters, letting them remain in a warm place. Let the liquid simmer to reduce. Make a sauce hollandaise. Let a very large iron skillet get very hot. Sprinkle some coarse salt upon it. Cook the steak thereon, searing each side at first, and then allowing it to cook 4 or 5 minutes on each side, the time depending upon the thickness of the steak. Add the reduced oyster liquor to the hollandaise and season with lemon juice, salt and pepper. Pour the sauce on a platter, lay on it the sizzling steak, cover with oysters, and serve at once.

★
## Beef Casserole with Beer

2 pounds rump steak
1 cut clove of garlic
3 slices good bacon
1 large onion
1 tablespoon sugar
2 cloves
1 bayleaf
6 to 8 peppercorns
Salt

[ 55 ]

3 tablespoons vinegar
Dark beer and water, half and half

Have steak cut rather thick. Beat it thoroughly with a rolling pin to break tissues. Massage it with garlic all over, then roll it up and tie with a string. Lay the bacon in a casserole. Add sliced onion, sugar, spices, and a sprinkle of salt. Lay in the meat, and pour the vinegar over it. Pour in enough beer and water, mixed in equal proportions, to cover the meat. The heat of the oven should be enough to have the liquid gently simmer (about 325°). Cook for 1½ to 2 hours. Thicken the sauce, if desired, with beurre manié. To serve, remove strings and place meat on a platter. Strain sauce over it, and serve the rest (strained) in a boat. Serves six.

★

## Beef Creole

2 pounds round steak, 1½ inches thick
1 tablespoon each lard and olive oil
2 large sliced onions
¼ cup tomato sauce
1 minced clove garlic
An herb bouquet
A pinch of saffron
1 teaspoon salt
Pepper

Cut meat in squares. Put lard and olive oil in a Dutch oven; add meat. Cover with onions, tomato sauce, garlic and seasonings. Cover, putting a piece of paper between lid and top of Dutch oven. Simmer very gently for 2 hours or until tender. Watch while cooking. There should be only a little gravy from the meat and onions. Serves four.

★
## Braised Oxtails

Cook as above, but brown oxtails in fat first, then cook for
4 or 5 hours; watch to see if a little water is needed.

★
## Estouffat of Beef

4 pounds beef in one compact piece (rump, chuck, or round)
3 tablespoons lard or beef fat
1 clove garlic, sliced
Minced truffles (optional)
1 pound small peeled carrots
½ pound small mushrooms
24 pitted black olives
1 diced sweet red pepper
1 quart red wine
2 teaspoons salt
Pepper
An herb bouquet

Brown the meat in the lard or fat, put in an enameled or
aluminum or earthenware casserole. (Do not use iron because
of the wine reaction.) Surround with vegetables, add other
ingredients, and cover, sealing the lid with a paste made of
flour and water. Cook in a 325° oven for 12 hours. You should
be able to cut the meat with a spoon. Serves six to eight.

## Gulyas

You will also find a recipe for Veal Gulyas in this book. Both
are good. In Hungary they eat it as a soup, with a spoon. Of
course there is more liquid when used this way.

3 pounds round or rump steak, sliced thick
2 medium onions
½ cup lard
2 teaspoons salt
1 tablespoon paprika
2 pounds tomatoes
1 pound peeled potatoes

Cut the meat in squares. Slice onions and brown with the meat in the lard. Add salt and paprika. Peel and seed tomatoes. Add, along with ¾ cup of water. Let come to a boil, reduce heat, cover and simmer for 1 hour. Add peeled and quartered potatoes and another ¾ cup of water. Continue simmering until potatoes and meat are tender. This recipe omits cream, but it can, of course, be added. Serves six to eight.

★

## Hamburgers

Get the BEST beef — enough for ½ pound per person. Pass it through the finest blade of the meat grinder. For each ½ pound, add 1 egg and ½ teaspoon of minced green onion. Add just enough fresh bread crumbs to sop up the egg — about ½ cup per pound of meat. Season with salt and pepper (allow 1 teaspoon of salt for each pound of meat). Form into large (½ pound) patties and brown in butter until good and hot through.

★

## Braised Shortribs

Such a dish was never even considered in my home as a child, and I only discovered its succulence when grown. There was a cafeteria on Market Street in San Francisco that excelled in shortribs, and I was frequently to be found enjoying the humble but excellent fare.

4 pounds shortribs
¼ cup olive oil
8 sliced onions
6 large peeled tomatoes
2 teaspoons salt
12 peppercorns
½ cup white wine
Flour

Have ribs cut in pieces. Brown in the olive oil and put in a Dutch oven. Brown onions in same fat until soft, and add to meat. Pour fat from the frying pan and swizzle the pan with the wine. Pour over meat, add salt and tomatoes and peppercorns. Cover and cook very slowly on top of the stove or in a 350° oven, adding liquid if necessary. With low heat and enough liquid, one need never fear too long cooking. Before serving, skim off all fat, correct seasoning, and if you think it necessary, thicken the sauce with a little flour. Serves six. If you wish, you can put 6 good-sized peeled potatoes in the pot 45 minutes to 1 hour before serving.

★

## Swiss Steak

2½ to 3 pounds thick round steak
Salt and pepper
Flour
2 tablespoons butter
2 tablespoons bacon fat
24 échalotes
2 slices thick bacon, diced

1 cup water
1 cup peeled, seeded, and diced tomatoes (optional)

Score meat lightly, season with salt and pepper, then pound into the meat as much flour as it will hold. Brown it in the fats. Slice échalotes and brown them with the bacon dice, using a Dutch oven or other pot with a cover. When nicely colored, lay on the meat, add a cup of water, cover tightly, and cook very slowly for 2 hours, or until meat is tender. The addition of a cup of peeled, seeded, and diced tomatoes is optional. I approve it. Serves six.

★

## Steak Tartare

This savory and robust recipe comes from the grill room of the Grand Hotel in Florence. Here it is prepared at the table by the maître d'hôtel, with as much ceremony as ever went with an order of crêpes Suzette.

> 1 pound best beef tenderloin
> 2 egg yolks
> 1 tablespoon (or more) finely minced onion
> 6 pounded anchovies
> ¼ to ½ cup finely minced parsley
> 2 tablespoons minced gherkins
> 1 tablespoon minced capers
> 2 teaspoons Worcestershire sauce
> 2 teaspoons lemon juice
> 2 tablespoons olive oil
> 1 teaspoon salt
> Freshly ground pepper

Chop the very finest fillet of beef by hand so that the result is a kind of purée. (If in a hurry, pass through the finest blade of the food chopper.) Add other ingredients and mix very well, until the color darkens. Form in a mound and let stand 15 minutes. Serve with thin slices or rye or pumpernickel, toasted or not.

★ NOTE: *The amounts of seasonings for beef tartare are more or less a matter of taste. If you want to mix it at the table, have the meat in a mound; make an indentation for the egg; surround with mounds of other ingredients except liquids, which can be on hand in cruets or pitchers. H.E.B.*

★

## Tournedos Rossini

Allow a rather thick tenderloin steak for each person; the same number of rather thick slices of bread, cut in rounds and fried in butter; and an equal number of slices of foie gras and of truffle. You also need butter, some beef stock or bouillon, and Madeira wine. Sauté the steaks in butter until done to your liking. Put each one on a round of bread, top with a rondelle (slice) of foie gras, and then with a slice of truffle. Keep the steaks warm while you add butter (if necessary) to the steak pan, a little stock and a little Madeira. Turn heat high and reduce volume by half. Pour over meat and serve at once. A noble Burgundy is indicated here.

Foie gras comes in cylindrical tins which are expressly made for such dishes as require rondelles of foie gras. They are certainly not cheap, but less expensive than the usual tins of truffled foie gras.

★

## Roast Beef

I once saw a French cook baste more than ½ pound of butter on a small piece of beef. It was prepared by the wife of a

[ 61 ]

Bonnétable café owner, and it was delicious. Try it if you are using a lower grade of beef, but it is not necessary for prime or choice beef, which has plenty of its own fat.

Select a standing rib roast or a sirloin roast, not too small. Sprinkle with salt and freshly ground pepper, and put into a 450° oven for 10 or 15 minutes. Reduce heat to 350° and roast until the meat thermometer reaches 120° if you like really rare beef, otherwise cook to your taste. If you have no meat thermometer, cook 12 to 15 minutes to the pound for very rare, although this isn't a safe gauge as a 4-rib roast and a 7-rib roast cook in about the same time, in spite of the difference in weight.

★

## Steak and Kidney Pie

How many times have I been grateful for this excellent recipe! It is universally appreciated; it is perfect for a buffet gathering, as it is what I call a "stretchable dish"; and if there is any left, it is wonderful the following day — almost even better than the first day. Welcome at any season, it is especially good in winter: a large casserole, steaming with succulent meats and sauces, is a heartwarming sight when one has come in from the cold out-of-doors. To proceed:

> 4 pounds top round steak, ¾ inch thick
> 6 veal kidneys
> ½ cup flour
> 3 tablespoons rendered beef fat
> 3 large onions, chopped
> 1 tablespoon Worcestershire sauce
> 1 tablespoon salt
> ¼ teaspoon pepper

Cut steak in 1½-inch squares. Remove cores and membranes from kidneys, and slice rather thin. Dredge beef with flour, rubbing it in well. Brown in the fat and put in a Dutch oven. Cover kidneys with cold water and bring just to the boil. Drain and repeat. Add to beef. Pour water into the pan in which you've browned the beef and scrape it out into the Dutch oven. Add onions, seasonings, and enough more water to cover the meat. Cover and simmer until just tender. Chill, put into a large casserole, and cover with a good pie crust, putting a little pitcher in the center to support the pastry. Make several slits for steam to escape, and bake in a hot oven (425°) until nicely browned.

★ NOTE: *Here I disagree with the author. I suspect he doesn't really like the flavor of kidneys. I tested it this way, and again by adding the raw sliced kidneys to the beef after that was cooked. I preferred the latter. It can also be made in the English way, by having both beef and kidneys put in the dish raw and cooked a longer time.* H.E.B.

★

## Grilled Kidneys

8 lamb kidneys
¼ cup olive oil
1 puréed clove garlic
Salt and freshly ground pepper
4 slices buttered toast

Split kidneys in half the long way and remove membrane and hard core. Marinate overnight in remaining ingredients (except toast); turn in the morning. Before serving time, skewer them flat and grill with high heat. Connoisseurs prefer them on the rarish side, as they toughen if cooked overly long. Serve them on the toast to catch the juices. Serves four.

[ 63 ]

★
## Mutton Chops Harvey

This recipe comes from Mrs. J. Downey Harvey, a celebrated San Francisco hostess whose table was second to none in California. Her mother, Mrs. B. B. Cutter, wrote a cookbook, *Practical Recipes* (1909), that is a collector's item.

> Double mutton chops (rib)
> Salt and pepper
> Cracker crumbs
> Slightly beaten egg
> Fat for deep frying
> Parsley

Buy enough chops for one per person, and have the butcher remove one bone from each chop and "French" the other one (scrape the meat from the end of it). Season well, dip in crumbs, then in egg, and again in crumbs. Heat fat to 370° and cook chops 3½ to 4 minutes; turn and cook the same on the other side. Serve on lots of beautiful springy parsley. Cold, these chops are absolutely perfect to take along on a picnic.

★
## Leg of Lamb à la Périgord

One of the most unusual recipes in this book, and one of the best.

> Small leg of lamb, about 5 to 6 pounds
> ¼ cup butter
> Salt and pepper
> 16 (at least) peeled garlic cloves
> 1½ cups white wine
> 1½ cups water
> ¼ cup Armagnac

Brown lamb in butter and season with salt and pepper; put in a pot with a cover. Add the whole peeled garlic cloves (more if you wish), wine and water. Put a heavy paper between lid and pot, and cook over the lowest possible heat for 3 hours. Turn the meat, add the Armagnac (Cognac could be used, but it's not authentic in this recipe), add more wine and water if necessary, but don't overdo. Cook, just as slowly, another 3 hours. Serve with small braised onions, small carrots, and potato balls. You need have no fear of the garlic — it will have cooked away, leaving a delicate but barely perceptible flavor. Dare and venture, and see how pleased you will be.

★

## Leg of Lamb with Pineapple

Leg of lamb
3 slices pineapple
2 tablespoons butter
3 sliced onions
3 sliced carrots
Salt and pepper
1 cup white port

Have bone removed from lamb. Split pineapple slices in half with a long sharp knife, then cut in slivers. Lift skin on lamb here and there and insert pineapple under it. Brown the meat in the butter, along with the vegetables. Sprinkle with salt and pepper, pour over the port, cover and cook gently for 3 hours, basting frequently.

★ NOTE: *This may also be roasted in a 350° oven. As I prefer my lamb on the pink side, I cook a considerably shorter time, until the meat thermometer reaches 140°. H.E.B.*

[ 65 ]

★
## Leg of Lamb à la Suédoise

This recipe, given me by Alfred Lunt, is one that has brought me such pleasure and success that I owe him eternal thanks. Joseph Oliver Tobin, one of San Francisco's celebrated epicures, told me that he considered this method of cooking lamb the very best, and Joe ought to know.

> Leg of lamb
> 2 cloves garlic
> 1½ tablespoons dry mustard
> 1½ tablespoons salt
> ¼ cup butter
> 1 cup water
> 1 cup strong coffee
> 2 lumps sugar
> ½ cup cream

Peel garlic and cut in needle-like slivers. Make gashes all over the meat, using a sharp-pointed knife, and insert garlic slivers. Rub all over with the mustard and salt, mixed together, massaging it into the flesh. Brown the meat in the butter, put in a roasting pan, add water, and bake in a 300° oven 30 minutes to the pound. When the meat is ¾ done, add the coffee, sugar, and cream. Baste from now on almost continually. Slice the roast rather thick. Pour gravy, slightly thickened with beurre manié, if you wish, over all.

★
## Old-Fashioned Boiled Mutton

This is from the cookbook of my grandmother, Mrs. George Brier.

Have the fell and gland removed from a leg of mutton, put

into a big pot with 12 peeled turnips, cover with boiling salted water, and simmer 15 minutes to the pound. Serve with caper sauce or Swedish horseradish sauce.

★

## Ham Baked with Milk

This is a very agreeable dish to have when one is away on summer vacations.

A very thick center slice of ham
3 tablespoons dry mustard
3 tablespoons light brown sugar
⅛ teaspoon ground cloves
Milk

Make a paste with mustard, brown sugar, cloves, and a few drops of milk. Spread over entire surface of ham. Put in a casserole and add milk to cover. Bake in a 325° oven for 1¼ hours. Serve with escalloped potatoes.

★

## Ham in Cream

6 slices cooked ham, ¼ inch thick
2 sliced onions
¼ cup butter
½ pound sliced mushrooms
1 teaspoon flour
1 cup cream
Salt and pepper
Rice

Have a good, well-flavored ham cut into small squares. Cook the onions in the butter until they begin to brown. Add the mushrooms and cook 4 or 5 minutes, then add the ham. Sim-

[ 67 ]

mer until the ham is cooked, add flour, stir, then pour in cream. Stir until hot and smooth. Correct seasonings and serve in a rice ring. Serves six.

★

## Baked Ham Virginia Style

This is from my grandmother's cookbook. She, no doubt, used an old-fashioned ham, cured with long smoking. In America I use a Virginia ham or *non*-tenderized one. In France I get a fine smoked ham from my charcutier, and in Italy I use a ham from Parma.

"Soak a medium-sized ham in cold water overnight. Then change the water, cover again, and when water comes to the boil, lower flame and let it just simmer 4 hours, adding more hot water if necessary. I speak now of old-fashioned, non-tenderized ham. When the bone looks loose, the ham is done. Some experts say 2 hours is quite enough for *any* ham. I don't agree to this, and find 3 hours for the average-sized ham just about right." I quote above my grandmother, but as she was a Virginian and always saw things in hospitably large quantities, her counsel for 4 hours may be because she had in mind something larger than a "medium-sized ham."

After the boiling, skin the ham. Score the fat, and then cover with bread crumbs and brown sugar. Put the ham in a pot containing 1 cup of the ham water, a small amount of brown sugar, and a pint of Madeira. Bake and baste often until the ham is well browned and the liquid is absorbed.

★

## Ham Mousse

½ pound cooked ham
½ pound raw veal

Salt and pepper
3 egg whites
2½ cups thick cream
Red coloring

Put the ham and veal through the finest blade of the meat grinder *three* times. Put in a bowl (in summer set in ice) and gradually mix in the egg whites. Then gradually mix in the cream. Add a little red food coloring; otherwise the mixture will be a rather unappetizing pale gray, so it is essential. Pour the mixture into a 5- or 6-cup buttered ring mold, cover with a buttered paper, put into a pan of hot water, and bake in a 300° oven until set. Cool slightly and unmold.

For mousse Eugénie, fill the center with sweetbreads covered with creamed mushrooms. It is an excellent lunch dish.

★ NOTE: *The ring mold must be very well buttered with cold butter. I find that sprinkling it with fine crumbs before adding the ham mixture facilitates unmolding.* H.E.B.

★

## Jambon Duc Charles

This delectable dish was a feature of the old restaurant Aux Trois Faisans in Dijon. The owner, M. Rocouchat, gave me the secret over a "fine" (Cognac) following a memorable lunch. This is a treasure.

1 pound sliced mushrooms
2 tablespoons butter
4 cups cream
⅓ cup Madeira
Pepper
8 slices cooked ham
3 or 4 ounces mousse de foie gras

Cook mushrooms in butter for 6 or 7 minutes, add cream, and simmer until thickened. Add Madeira, pepper, and salt if needed. Spread ham with foie gras, fold over, and arrange on a baking dish. Add sauce and cook in a 350° oven for a very few minutes — just long enough to heat thoroughly and allow the foie gras to melt a trifle. Serves eight.

★

## Roast Pork in Milk

This is an Italian recipe.

> A 6-rib roast of pork (may be from the loin)
> Salt and pepper
> Milk
> 6 or 8 slices of bread, fried

Trim off any excess fat and sprinkle pork with salt and pepper. Put in a deep casserole and add enough milk to come halfway up the pork. Cover and roast in a 350° oven, basting occasionally, and turning when the meat is half cooked. When done (about 2 hours) the roast will be brown on top and the milk will have largely cooked away. Put fried bread on a platter, arrange roast on it, and pour pan gravy around. It will be tender and delicious. Serve with a purée of potatoes to four or six.

★

## Baked Pork Spareribs

Cut spareribs into properly sized pieces, then put them on a rack in a moderate oven for 20 minutes or half an hour to extract fat. Now spread them with a mixture of dry mustard, tomato catsup, and orange marmalade. Return to the oven for half an hour or so, until they are crusty. Salt them lightly and baste frequently during the process. Be sure to have finger bowls with warm water, and large paper napkins, for it is more practical to eat spareribs with the fingers.

★

## Scrapple

I include this recipe for two reasons. One, I cannot buy it already made in Europe, and this is an excellent formula. Two, my father always insisted, anyway, that the bought kind usually had a large content of sawdust in its making. I owe thanks to Helen Evans Brown for the base of this scrapple, with an addition or two of my own, but I have confessed to that delightful and wonderful cook of the liberties that I have taken!

This quantity will fill one loaf pan. Cook 2 fresh pigs' feet along with a pound of pork shoulder in a quart of boiling water and 2 teaspoons of salt, until the meat can be easily picked from the bones. When you have done this, and have strained the broth into a saucepan, grind the meat. To the broth add ¼ cup of chopped onion and ¾ cup of corn meal. Cook this for 2 minutes, then add meat, 10 peppercorns, and ½ teaspoon of orégano, with more salt and pepper if need be. Cook the mixture until thick, then pour into a loaf pan and set aside to chill. Slice and fry before serving. The scrapple will keep a week or so in the refrigerator, and makes a most excellent base for shepherd's pie, too.

★

## Curried Sausages

Allow 4 or 5 pork sausages per person. Prick them all over with a basting needle, so they will not burst in the heat, and bake them in the oven. When cooked, put 2 tablespoons of sausage fat in a skillet, stirring in 1 tablespoon of flour. Add to the fat and flour a tablespoon of curry powder, letting the mixture simmer 2 or 3 minutes. Then add a cup of boiling water and let cook gently for 15 minutes before you throw in the sausages. Serve with boiled rice.

★

## Sausages in White Wine

Procure long pork sausages. Prick them copiously with a basting needle and arrange in a flat earthenware baking dish. Pour over them a glass or two of white wine, and put into a very hot (450°) oven for 10 minutes. Then pour off the sauce, skim off fat, and add a little stock. Pour this over the sausages and serve with a purée of potatoes.

★

## Albondigas

This was born in Mexico, educated in San Francisco.

The first time I tasted albondigas, I was with a friend whose two children asked what we were having for lunch. When their mother pronounced the word "albondigas," the air was rent with ecstatic squeals of childish joy. After partaking, I could well understand such exuberance, and, indeed, share it (minus the squeals).

> 2 pounds finely chopped veal
> 4 cups soft bread crumbs
> Milk
> 2 teaspoons salt
> Pepper
> 2 eggs
> Flour
> 1 large onion, chopped
> 1 green pepper, chopped

2 tablespoons butter
1 No. 2½ can tomatoes
Salt and pepper
Orégano

Mix veal, crumbs, slightly moistened with milk, salt, pepper, and eggs. Form into fairly large balls and roll in flour. Brown onion and green pepper in butter; add tomatoes, and season to taste with salt, pepper, and orégano. Lay the meat balls on top, cover, and cook very slowly for an hour, turning once or twice. Serves six.

★

## Veal à la Béchamel

Good for a simple Sunday supper or summer lunch.

¾ pound finely ground veal
¼ pound finely ground pork
1½ cups dried bread crumbs
½ cup milk
1½ teaspoons salt
Pepper
3 échalotes, chopped
1 tablespoon butter
2 eggs
Flour
2 cups Béchamel sauce
2 egg yolks
Parsley

Mix veal, pork, bread crumbs, milk, salt and pepper to taste. Cook échalotes in butter until soft, and add, along with eggs. Mix well and form into small balls, roll in flour, and poach in salted water for 20 minutes. Drain well and arrange on a flat dish. Heat Béchamel, beat a little into the egg yolks, and then beat egg mixture into remainder of sauce. Pour over veal balls and serve, sprinkled with minced parsley. Serves four.

★

## Blanquette de Veau

2 pounds young white veal
2 carrots
1 teaspoon salt
Pepper
An herb bouquet
1 tablespoon butter
1 tablespoon flour
2 egg yolks
1 teaspoon lemon juice
2 teaspoons butter

Cut the veal into small squares, add carrots and seasonings and herbs, and almost cover with water. Simmer very slowly until tender — about 1¼ hours. Make a roux with butter and flour, add 2 cups of the veal stock, strained, and reduce to 1½ cups. Beat a little sauce into the egg yolks; then beat the mixture into the rest of the sauce and add lemon juice and butter. Cook until smooth (don't boil), add meat, correct seasoning, and serve with parsley potatoes. Serves four.

★ NOTE: *This sauce should be thin, but if it's too thin add 1 more egg yolk or a teaspoon of beurre manié.* H.E.B.

★

## Brézolles

6 veal escalopes
2 tablespoons olive oil
¼ cup minced chervil

¼ cup minced chives
¼ cup minced parsley
1 tablespoon minced tarragon
4 minced échalotes
1 minced clove garlic
1 teaspoon salt
Pepper
4 thin slices bacon
Flour
½ cup dry white Bordeaux

The veal should be sliced very thin and the pieces not too large — they will serve six persons. Put olive oil in an earthenware casserole and add a layer of the veal. Mix the herbs, échalotes, and garlic with salt and pepper, and sprinkle a layer over the meat. Repeat until the ingredients are used. Top with bacon, seal the cover on with a flour and water paste, and cook in a 350° oven for 45 minutes. Warm the wine and pour over all; cover and cook another 30 minutes. Remove bacon and fat from casserole. Correct seasoning and serve from the casserole, with boiled potatoes or pommes château.

★

## Veau à la Crème

This recipe is from the Restaurant La Louve in Nîmes, France. It is for a single portion, but can be increased quite easily.

Sauté a lightly floured escalope of veal and ¼ cup of sliced mushrooms in 2 tablespoons of butter until lightly browned. Sprinkle with salt and pepper; add ½ cup of white wine, stirring so that the brown bits in the pan are loosened. After 5 minutes, stir in ½ cup of heavy cream, reheat and serve.

★

## Cold Veal with Tuna Mayonnaise
### (*Vitella Tonnato Monte Pincio*)

This is extremely good for a summer lunch.

Cold sliced veal — enough for four or six
1 7-ounce tin tuna, packed in olive oil
1½ cups mayonnaise
1 tablespoon capers
1 tablespoon lemon juice

Arrange veal on a platter with the slices overlapping. Pound the tuna to a paste and mix it with the mayonnaise (or whirl them together in an electric blender); add the capers and lemon juice. Pour some of the tuna mayonnaise over the meat and pass the rest. Arrange lettuce nests with string bean salad on either side of the meat, and garnish with anchovy fillets.

★

## Veal Chops en Papillotes

8 veal chops
6 tablespoons olive oil
2 tablespoons minced parsley
2 tablespoons minced chives
4 chopped échalotes
1 pound chopped mushrooms
¼ pound butter
¼ cup chopped raw ham (optional)
8 sheets good bond typewriter paper

Cover veal chops with olive oil and let stand overnight; turn in the morning. Mix parsley, chives and échalotes. Sauté mushrooms in 3 tablespoons of butter and mix with the herbs (¼ cup of chopped raw ham may also be added). Butter the paper. In the center of each put a layer of the herb-mushroom mixture. Top with a chop and cover with more mixture. Put a teaspoon of butter on top of each chop, fold the paper over it and seal the edges with a double fold. Bake in a 375° oven for 45 minutes. Serve in the wrappers, cutting the top paper with a pair of sharp-pointed scissors. Serves eight.

★

### Veal Cutlets Portugaise

> 8 uniform veal escalopes
> 3 tablespoons olive oil
> 2 minced échalotes
> 1 clove garlic, puréed
> 4 peeled and seeded tomatoes
> Salt and pepper
> 1 tablespoon minced parsley
> ½ cup veal stock or consommé

Sauté veal in olive oil until golden. Add échalotes and garlic, cook a couple of minutes, then add tomatoes, cut in quarters. Add salt and pepper to taste, parsley and stock. Cover pot or casserole, sealing with flour and water paste, and bake in a 350° oven for 35 minutes. Serve with a pilaf of rice. Serves eight.

★

### Escalopes in "Sandwiches"

The "sandwich" filling is ham and bacon.

> 6 escalopes of tender veal
> 3 slices ham
> 3 slices bacon
> ¼ cup butter

[ 77 ]

2 cups bouillon
2 cups puréed mushrooms

Cut each escalope in two the long way. Cut ham and bacon in two. Put a slice of ham and one of bacon on a veal piece, and top with another slice of veal. The "sandwich" should be neat, so trim if necessary. Tie with thread and brown in butter, then add bouillon and cook gently over a low flame for an hour or until tender. To serve, cut sandwiches in two, remove threads, and serve with creamed mushrooms. Serves six.

★

## Veal Cutlets à la Foyot

To many epicures, Foyot's, across the street from the Luxembourg Palace in Paris, was the greatest and certainly the most dignified of all the great restaurants. It was truly a temple of gastronomy, where people went to savor food raised to the nth degree of perfection. And got it! I have always felt a personal sense of indignation that Paris let this wonderful place disappear. It should have been subsidized by the government as a Monument Historique et Gastronomique! As, indeed, the mansion in which it was situated *was* a national monument.

Brown 2 rather thick veal cutlets in butter, then salt and pepper them. Pour in dry white wine to half the height of the meat; cook quickly until wine is evaporated. Meanwhile, cook ½ pound of sliced mushrooms in 2 tablespoons of butter, seasoning with salt and pepper and the juice of a lemon. Then, this achieved, pour all over the veal. Sprinkle generously with grated Gruyère cheese, and bake about 20 minutes. Serves four.

★
## Veal Gulyas

1 thick slice bacon
¼ cup olive oil
5 large sliced onions
2 pounds veal steak, sliced ¾ inch thick
1 teaspoon salt
1 tablespoon flour
1 tablespoon paprika
1 cup sweet or sour cream

Cube the bacon and cook until the fat is rendered. Add olive oil and onions; cook until onions are softened. Cut the meat in large squares, sprinkle with salt, and add to pan. When the meat has browned, sprinkle with flour and turn; add paprika and turn again. Cover with boiling water, cover and simmer until tender — about 1½ hours. Add cream or sour cream; heat. Correct seasoning and thicken with a little flour or cornstarch, if desired. Serve with noodles. Serves four.

★
## Veal and Ham Loaf

1½ pounds raw veal
1 pound ham
2 eggs
1 cup milk
1 cup cracker crumbs
1¼ teaspoons salt
Freshly ground pepper
¾ cup brown sugar
1 teaspoon paprika
¼ cup hot water
1 tablespoon dry mustard
2 tablespoons vinegar

[ 79 ]

Put meat through grinder, using fine blade. Add eggs, milk, crumbs, salt and pepper, and mix well. Mold into a loaf or put in a loaf pan, and bake in a 375° oven, basting with the remaining ingredients mixed together. This will take about one hour and will serve eight.

★

### Veal Kidneys en Cocotte

4 or 5 veal kidneys with fat
2 tablespoons chopped bacon
½ pound sliced mushrooms
Salt and pepper

Have ½ inch of fat left on the outside of the kidneys. Put in a skillet with bacon and mushrooms, and cook until browned. Season with salt and pepper. Put in a casserole, cover, and cook in a 375° to 400° oven for a half-hour, basting occasionally. To serve, cut into slices, fat and all. Serve with pommes noisettes, braised tiny white onions, and buttered baby carrots. Serves eight.

★

### Veal Kidneys in Cream Sauce

½ cup chopped onion
¼ cup butter
1 cup veal stock or consommé
2 veal kidneys
Salt, pepper, paprika
¼ pound mushrooms, sliced thin
1 cup cream
1 teaspoon vinegar
1 teaspoon grated horseradish

Cook onions in half the butter until wilted. Add stock and simmer. Remove core and membrane from kidneys, and slice. Sprinkle with seasonings and brown in remaining butter. Remove from pan, and in same butter cook mushrooms; when lightly browned add cream, vinegar and horseradish. Combine all and heat, but do not boil. Serve with rice. Serves three or four.

*

### Veal Kidneys à l'Indienne

¼ pound mushrooms
Butter
2 cups veal stock
2 tablespoons flour
6 veal kidneys
1 teaspoon curry powder
1 cup cream
2 egg yolks
Salt and pepper

Chop mushrooms, cook in 1 tablespoon of butter, then add 1 cup of the stock and simmer 1 hour. Force through a sieve. Make a roux of 2 tablespoons of butter and the flour. Add remaining stock and cook until thick and smooth; keep warm. Slice the kidneys and sauté in 2 tablespoons of butter for 5 minutes; add curry, mix well and keep warm. Add mushrooms to sauce and bring to a boil. Remove from heat, add cream mixed with yolks, then reheat gently; do not boil. Add salt and pepper to taste. Put kidneys on a platter, pour sauce over, and serve to six.

★

## Veal Kidneys Prooce

Dedicated to Gabrielle Rives, with love.

> 8 baby veal kidneys
> ½ cup butter
> Salt and pepper
> 1 tablespoon dry mustard
> Juice of 1 lemon

If you can't find baby veal kidneys, use 4 larger ones; slice them. Put half the butter in a skillet and in it cook the kidneys only long enough to sear the outside. Season with salt and pepper and keep warm, but don't allow to cook further or they will toughen. Add remaining butter to another skillet (not an iron or steel one) and stir in mustard. Blend in juices from the other skillet, stirring constantly. Add lemon juice, correct seasoning, and heat. Add kidneys and serve with flaky rice. Serves eight.

★

## Stuffed Veal Kidneys

> 4 veal kidneys
> 2 sets lamb brains or 1 set veal brains
> ¼ pound bacon
> Butter
> ¼ pound chopped mushrooms
> 2 teaspoons minced parsley
> 1 egg
> Salt and pepper
> 2 cups veal stock or consommé
> ¼ cup sherry
> Beurre manié

Split kidneys almost in half the long way, leaving a little "hinge." Soak brains in cold water, clean of membranes, and parboil in salted water for 15 minutes; cool and chop. Chop the bacon and cook it in 1 tablespoon of butter until fat is rendered. Add mushrooms, cook 5 or 6 minutes, add parsley, brains, egg, and salt and pepper to taste. Stuff kidneys with mixture and tie with thread. Cook carefully in ¼ cup of butter, turning frequently, until brown. Add stock and sherry, cover and simmer until done to your liking (or put in a casserole and bake in a 350° oven. Thicken sauce slightly with beurre manié, and serve to eight.

★

### Calf Liver en Papillotes

8 thick slices calf liver
Flour
Butter
16 thin slices bacon
¼ cup minced parsley
8 échalotes, minced
Salt and pepper
8 sheets good bond typewriter paper

Dredge liver lightly with flour and sear in ¼ cup of butter (don't *cook*). Butter the paper very generously. Put a slice of bacon on each, sprinkle with minced parsley and échalotes, lay on a slice of liver, salt and pepper lightly, add a small piece of butter and more herbs. Top with another piece of bacon. Fold edges with a double fold (if necessary fasten with paper clips), and put in a 350° oven for 30 minutes. Serve in the paper, cutting top out with sharp-pointed scissors. Serves eight.

[ 83 ]

★

## Liver Soufflé

1 pound calf liver
¼ cup butter
½ cup thick Béchamel sauce
3 eggs, separated
½ cup whipping cream
1 teaspoon salt
Pepper
Sauce Madère

Sauté liver in butter, then mash it thoroughly in a mortar or, *faute de mieux,* pass it three times through the fine blade of the food chopper. Add Béchamel, which must be cold; the egg yolks, well beaten; the cream, whipped; salt and pepper. Mix well. Beat the egg whites stiff and fold in. Put into a well-buttered 3-pint soufflé dish and bake in a 350° oven about 30 minutes. Serve with sauce Madère. Serves four.

★

## Veal Marengo

This recipe is from the Comtesse de Vigneral, of Paris.

3 pounds boneless veal shoulder
Flour
Salt and pepper
¼ cup butter
1 cup chopped onion
1 pound tomatoes, peeled and seeded
1½ cups white wine
1 clove garlic, puréed
1 herb bouquet
Minced parsley

[ 84 ]

Cut the veal in rather large pieces, dust with flour, season with salt and pepper, and brown in the butter. Set aside. Cook the chopped onions in the same butter; add the tomatoes, wine, garlic and herb bouquet. Return the veal to the mixture and simmer until it is tender and the sauce is reduced — about 1½ hours. Correct seasoning, put meat on a platter, sieve the sauce and pour over. Sprinkle with parsley and serve with rice and a purée of spinach. Serves eight.

★

## Paprika Schnitzel

3 thinly sliced onions
¼ cup butter
2 tablespoons good paprika
Salt and pepper
8 small veal steaks, ½ inch thick
1½ cups sour cream

Cook onions in butter until wilted; sprinkle with paprika, salt and pepper, and stir until a deep red. Draw onions to one side of the pan (or remove), and brown meat in the same pan. Spoon onions over meat, add sour cream, and cook over very low heat for ½ hour, adding a very little water if necessary. The meat should be tender and the liquid reduced. Correct seasoning and serve to eight.

★

## Sweetbreads à la Ali Bab

This famous authority gives us this recipe. It is for two persons.

1 pair sweetbreads
¼ cup butter
½ cup minced onion

[ 85 ]

½ cup minced carrot
An herb bouquet
1 cup consommé
Salt and pepper

Soak sweetbreads in salted water 30 minutes, then remove membranes. Dry, and brown in butter for 15 minutes. Remove from pan and replace with onions, carrots, and herb bouquet. Cook slowly for 15 minutes; they will stick slightly to the pan, but be careful they don't burn. Add the sweetbreads, consommé and salt and pepper to taste. Cover and cook gently for 30 minutes. Skim off fat and serve with little peas.

★

## Sweetbread Croquettes

This recipe is from my grandmother's cookbook.

1 pound sweetbreads
1 tablespoon salt
1 tablespoon lemon juice
Cooked breast of one chicken
½ cup dry bread crumbs
1 cup thick cream
Salt, pepper and nutmeg
Egg
Cracker crumbs
Deep fat for frying

Cover sweetbreads with water, add salt and lemon juice, and bring to a boil. Turn heat low and simmer 20 minutes. Plunge the sweetbreads into cold water, clean, and cut in small dice. Grind the chicken breast, using the fine blade of the meat chopper; add to sweetbreads. Soak crumbs in cream and stir to a smooth paste (or use 1½ cups thick cream sauce). Season with salt, pepper, and grated nutmeg to taste; mix with sweetbreads and chicken, and chill. Form into croquettes, roll in cracker crumbs, dip in slightly beaten egg, and again in crumbs. Fry in deep fat at 370° until nicely browned. Serve with mushroom sauce and fresh peas. Serves six.

★

## Sweetbreads au Jus

3 pairs sweetbreads
1 cup diced bacon
2 cups thinly sliced carrots
2 thinly sliced onions
¼ cup butter
Salt and pepper
2 cups consommé
2 tablespoons minced parsley

Soak sweetbreads in cold water 30 minutes, clean and let come to a boil in salted water. Drain, dry, remove membranes, and put on a plate. Cover with another plate with a weight on top (canned goods make fine weights). Brown carrots and onions in bacon. Brown sweetbreads in butter and sprinkle with salt and pepper. Put vegetables and bacon in the bottom of a casserole, top with the sweetbreads, rinse sweetbread pan with the consommé, and pour over all. Sprinkle with parsley, cover, and bake in a 350° oven for 30 minutes. Serves six.

★

## Sweetbreads Normande

Échalotes, mushrooms, Calvados and cream! What could be more redolent of Normandy? This recipe comes from the Hostellerie du Vieux Logis, Gerberoy, Oise.

4 pairs sweetbreads
6 échalotes, minced

[ 87 ]

¼ cup butter
½ pound mushrooms, sliced
Salt and pepper
½ cup Calvados
1 teaspoon glace de viande
1 cup cream

Cook and press sweetbreads, as for sweetbreads au jus. Sauté échalotes in butter, slice the sweetbreads and add. When nearly done but not brown, add the mushrooms and salt and pepper to taste, and cook 3 minutes. Pour on Calvados and light, basting until the flames die down. Add glace de viande, then stir in cream. Heat and serve with sliced fried apples. Serves eight.

★

## *Veal Tongue*

A baby veal tongue is inexpensive and delicious. One is large enough for two or three persons.

1 veal tongue
3 carrots
1 clove garlic, peeled
An herb bouquet
1 tablespoon salt
Pepper
4 onions
4 whole cloves
2 tablespoons butter
2 tablespoons flour
1 pound peeled seeded tomatoes
Herbs
Boiled noodles

Cover tongue with water and add carrots, garlic, herb bouquet, salt, pepper, and 2 of the onions stuck with the cloves. Simmer 2½ to 3 hours, or until tender. Remove skin and return tongue to broth to cool. Slice remaining onions and cook in butter until wilted. Add flour and tomatoes, and simmer 30 minutes. Add enough tongue broth to thin, season to taste with salt, pepper, and herbs of your choice — basil or tarragon is nice. Slice meat, put on a bed of hot noodles, and cover with sauce.

★

## Veal Tongue with Raisin and Almond Sauce

    1 cooked veal tongue
    ¼ cup butter
    2 tablespoons flour
    1 teaspoon glace de viande, or 1 bouillon cube
    Pepper and salt
    Juice of ½ lemon
    Pinch of sugar
    ¼ cup seedless raisins
    3 tablespoons chopped blanched almonds

Cook tongue as in preceding recipe, but cut time to 2 hours. Peel and cut in slices. Make a roux with butter and flour, add 1 cup of broth from the tongue, glace de viande, a grinding of pepper, lemon juice, sugar, raisins, nuts, and salt to taste. Simmer tongue slices in this for 45 minutes, or until tender. Serve with rice. Serves two or three.

CHICKEN,
POULTRY
and
GAME
BIRDS

A DON VIVA'S COOKBOOK

Chicken à la Chivette

★
## *Boiled Chicken with Tarragon*

                4- to 5-pound roasting chicken
                Tarragon
                Salt pork, sliced paper-thin
                2 teaspoons salt
                ¼ teaspoon pepper
                Herb bouquet
                2 sliced carrots
                1 large sliced onion
                3 egg yolks

Truss the fowl for roasting, after putting in the cavity a
large handful of tarragon, or 2 teaspoons of dried tarragon.
Close the vent. Place salt pork on the breast and tie it. Make
a court bouillon of salt, pepper, herb bouquet, tarragon sprigs,
carrots, onion, and enough water to cover the chicken. Bring
to the boil and put the bird in. Simmer until tender (about 1
to 1¼ hours); do not boil. Then remove the chicken and drain
well. Strain the liquid and reduce to 5 cups. Beat egg yolks
slightly and add some of the hot stock, then beat the mixture
into remainder of the stock and cook very gently until thickened. (If sauce isn't thick enough, a teaspoon or two of cornstarch mixed with a little cold water may be added.) Remove
salt pork from chicken breast and decorate with a few whole
leaves of tarragon. Put on a platter and pour sauce around.
Serves four.

★

## Chicken à la Cocotte

Put ½ cup of butter in a cocotte and carefully brown the outside of a trussed tender young chicken. Salt, then cover the cocotte and let the chicken cook very gently until barely tender. When done, turn up the flame, uncover, and brown the bird consistently. Remove strings from the bird and serve, pouring juices over.

★

## Roast Little Chickens

Many years ago this recipe was sent to me by Mrs. Maude, and I have always been grateful for it. Allow very small chickens, one for each person (squab chickens), or use broilers, allowing one for each two persons. Chop chicken livers, allowing 1 for each small bird, and stew in 2 tablespoons of butter, a tablespoon each of ham, parsley and fresh bread crumbs (double these amounts if broilers are used). Season with salt and pepper, and stuff the birds with this. Truss, brush with olive oil, and sprinkle with paprika. Roast in a 350° oven — 35 minutes for small birds, up to an hour for larger ones. Serve on large croûtons of fried bread.

★

## Chicken Breasts with White Truffles

This prize dish comes from Doney's Restaurant, one of the best in Florence.

> 4 whole chicken breasts
> Flour, salt and pepper
> ¼ cup butter (or more)
> ½ cup Cognac

1 cup heavy cream
1 or 2 white truffles

Separate breasts, removing bones. Dust with flour and season with salt and pepper. Sauté in the butter until colored, adding more butter if necessary. Add Cognac, light, and let the flames die down. Then add cream, cover and cook over very low heat until tender. Slice the truffle (or truffles) very thin, add to the sauce, and cook a minute or two before serving with a purée of potatoes. Serves six to eight.

★

## Chicken Flambé with Grapes

4- to 5-pound roasting chicken
Salt and pepper
About ¾ cup (1½ bars) melted butter
1 cup peeled seedless Malaga grapes
½ glass Malaga wine
½ cup water
½ cup Cognac

Salt and pepper the chicken, inside and out. Truss. Put 2 tablespoons butter in a roasting pan, put the chicken in breast side down, and put in a 400° oven. As the bird begins to brown, start basting it with ½ cup of butter. Reduce heat to 350° and turn the bird to brown on all sides, basting every 5 minutes until the chicken has a grand look. Make a sauce by simmering together the peeled grapes, Malaga wine, ½ cup of water, and a tablespoon of butter. Simmer a couple of minutes. Place chicken on a warm platter, pour grape sauce around it, pour Cognac over it, light, and take to the table for all to enjoy the flaming triumph.

★ NOTE: *It hurts my occasionally thrifty soul to waste the good juices and butter in the pan, so I add them to the sauce. If Malaga grapes are unavailable use seedless or even canned Muscats. A mellow sherry can be used instead of the Malaga wine.* H.E.B.

★

## Chickens with Cognac and Port

2 young chickens
¼ cup butter
12 peeled échalotes
⅛ cup Cognac
3 cups cream
Salt and pepper
1 8-ounce tin button mushrooms
    or 1 pound small fresh mushrooms
½ glass port wine

Have chickens disjointed — use backs for stock — and brown other pieces and the échalotes in butter. (Don't disregard the wings; they are a very tasty morsel, even when tiny.) When beautifully colored, add the Cognac and the cream. Season with salt and pepper, and simmer 20 minutes. Drain the mushrooms (or sauté fresh ones) and add the port to them. Simmer 10 minutes. Combine the two mixtures, reheat, and serve to eight.

★

## Coq au Vin

Is it necessary to say that coq au vin is one of the greatest culinary triumphs that has come from Burgundy, that source of so many incredibly inspired things to eat?

½ pound salt pork
¼ cup butter
12 small peeled white onions

1 chicken, cut in pieces
1 small clove garlic, puréed
An herb bouquet
Salt and pepper
12 large mushrooms, sliced
¼ cup Cognac
2 cups red Burgundy
Beurre manié

Dice salt pork, put in an earthenware casserole with butter and onions, and cook until the onions are brown. (★ NOTE: *Use an asbestos mat under your casserole, or use an enameled or stainless steel one that will stand direct heat.* H.E.B.) Brown chicken in same fat, remove excess grease, and add garlic, herb bouquet, salt and pepper, mushrooms, and Cognac. Heat enough to light the Cognac, and when the flames die down, add wine, cover, and simmer until the chicken is tender. This may be done in a 350° oven, if preferred. In either case, it should take under an hour. Correct seasoning, thicken sauce slightly with beurre manié, and serve with crusty bread and a red Burgundy. Serves four.

★
## Chicken and Veal Croquettes

2 small chickens
2 pounds boneless veal
1½ cups Béchamel sauce
3 teaspoons salt
¼ teaspoon pepper
Fine cracker crumbs
Slightly beaten egg
½ cup butter (or more)
3 cups heavy cream

[ 97 ]

Remove bones and skin from chicken, and gristle and fat from veal. Grind together twice, using the finest blade of the meat grinder. Mix with the sauce and seasonings; form into cutlets (chop-shaped pieces, ½ inch thick) or into cakes. Dust with cracker crumbs, dip in egg, and again roll in cracker crumbs. Let stand a few minutes (or longer) and sauté in butter until golden on both sides. (Add more butter if necessary.) Don't overcook. When done, remove to a hot platter and pour the cream into the pan. Turn heat high and cook 2 or 3 minutes. (Thicken with beurre manié, if you wish, but it shouldn't be needed.) Strain over croquettes and serve. Serves eight.

★

## Chicken Hash with Sausage

3- or 4-pound roast chicken
3 tablespoons butter
4 tablespoons flour
2½ cups cream
1 small tin shoestring pimientos
1 tablespoon minced parsley
Salt and pepper
1½ pounds link pork sausage

Remove meat from chicken and cut in small neat dice. Make sauce with butter and flour, cream, a tablespoon of the pimientos, and the parsley. Season to taste with salt and pepper; add the chicken and simmer very slowly. Prick the sausages with a fork and cook slowly over low heat until brown. Put chicken hash in the middle of a platter and surround with the sausages. Use remaining pimiento to garnish the chicken. Serve with baked potatoes and carrots Vichy. Serves six.

★ NOTE: *This "hash" may be different from the one you know, but it is classic. Also wonderful topped with poached eggs, for breakfast.* H.E.B.

★
## Chicken Liver Ring

½ pound chicken livers
5 eggs
1 cup cream
1 teaspoon salt
Butter and crumbs to coat mold
1 pound button mushrooms
¼ cup butter
¼ cup flour
1 cup cream
1 cup sour cream
Salt and pepper
¼ cup minced parsley

Soak the chicken livers in cold water 30 minutes, drain, pick over, and run through the fine blade of the meat grinder. Slightly beat the eggs; add cream and salt. Butter a 4- to 5-cup ring mold with *cold* butter and dust with fine crumbs. Combine livers with egg mixture and mix well. Strain liver mixture into prepared mold, set mold in a larger pan, and fill pan with enough hot water to come halfway up the sides of the mold. Put in a 350° oven for 35 minutes, or until an inserted knife comes out clean. In the meantime, cut ends from mushroom stems and cook in the butter for 6 or 7 minutes. Sprinkle with flour, add cream, cook a few minutes until thick and smooth, then fold in sour cream. Do not allow to boil after sour cream is added. Season with salt and pepper, and add parsley. Unmold liver ring on a serving plate, fill with mushrooms, and serve. This will serve six generously, eight if used as a first course.

★ NOTE: *A far easier and less messy way to make the liver ring is to whirl all ingredients smooth in an electric blender.* H.E.B.

★
## Chicken Marengo

1 minced clove garlic
2 onions, chopped
¼ cup olive oil
1 4-pound chicken, cut in pieces
Salt and pepper
1 pound mushrooms
3 sprigs parsley
3 échalotes
½ cup white wine
½ cup tomato purée
Fried croûtons

Cook the garlic and chopped onions in the olive oil until they begin to color. Sprinkle chicken with salt and pepper, and add to same pan, and cook for 45 minutes, turning to brown on all sides. Chop the mushrooms, along with the parsley and échalotes, which have been minced, and add. Add wine and tomato purée. Cover and simmer another 15 minutes, or until chicken is tender. Correct seasoning, arrange chicken on a platter, pour sauce over it, and garnish with small fried croûtons. Serves four.

★ NOTE: *Escoffier said the croûtons should be heart-shaped, and that fried eggs, too, should garnish the platter. The latter, I think, could be dispensed with.* H.E.B.

★
## Chicken Mousse

1 4- or 5-pound chicken
2 onions, sliced
2 carrots, sliced
2 leeks, sliced
2 celery ribs, sliced
Herb bouquet
2 teaspoons salt
6 peppercorns
1 envelope plain gelatine
¼ cup cold water
4 eggs, separated
1 cup whipping cream

Cover chicken with cold water and add vegetables and seasonings. Bring to a boil, turn heat low, and simmer until the chicken is just tender. Take care not to overcook — the breast should be juicy, not dry and stringy. Cool, remove meat from bones, and grind, using the finest blade. You'll want 2 cups of meat, preferably breast, so start with breast and wings. Soften gelatine in cold water and add to 2 cups of strained hot broth in which the chicken was cooked. Cool, and when it begins to thicken, add the egg yolks, beaten thick, and the chicken. Taste for seasoning, remembering that the cream and egg whites are still to come. Whip cream, beat egg whites stiff, and fold into the mixture. Pour into a 2-quart mold moistened with cold water, and refrigerate until set. Turn out on a pretty plate and garnish with cress or lettuce. Serves eight.

★
## Oignonade à la Bretonne

2 quarts pickling onions
½ cup (1 bar) butter
12 chicken breasts (from 6 chickens)
Salt and pepper
½ pound sautéed sliced mushrooms
¼ cup glace de veau (see Note)
2 cups heavy cream

Peel the tiny onions and cook them in butter until tender but not brown. Put half of them in a shallow baking dish. Cover with the breasts of chicken, sprinkle generously with salt and pepper, and add remaining onions, then cover with the mushrooms, which have been sautéed in a little butter. Mix glace de veau with cream and pour over all. Cook in a 350° oven for 30 minutes, or until hot and bubbly. Serve with peas and a purée of potatoes. Serves six to twelve, depending upon whether you allow one or two breasts to a person.

★ NOTE: *Peeling the onions is a less tearful project if you parboil them for 3 or 4 minutes before peeling. Glace de veau is veal stock, reduced to a glaze. A good substitute is to reduce a can of consommé to ¼ cup.* H.E.B.

★
## Chicken in Crêpes

2 minced onions
½ minced green pepper
2 minced celery ribs
½ pound thinly sliced mushrooms
½ cup butter
2 cups finely diced cooked chicken

Salt, pepper, tarragon
2 cups sauce Mornay

Cook vegetables in butter until soft. Add chicken, salt, pepper, and tarragon to taste. Divide among crêpes, tuck in sides, and roll up. Arrange on a flat serving dish, cover with sauce Mornay, and cook in a 350° oven until hot and brown. Serves eight.

★

## Crêpes

1 cup milk
2 eggs
¼ cup melted butter
½ cup flour
¾ teaspoon salt

Beat all together until smooth (an electric blender is quick and easy). Brush a hot 6- or 7-inch crêpe or omelette pan with butter, add a thin layer of batter (about 1½ tablespoons), and turn and tip so that it runs smoothly over the bottom of the pan. Cook on one side only, then slide onto plate until all are done. Makes about 24 crêpes.

★ NOTE: *These crêpes are very tender; delicious for desserts, too, in which case add 2 teaspoons of sugar and a table- spoon of Cognac.* H.E.B.

★

## Poule au Pot Henri IV

1 large roasting chicken
1 chopped onion
2 tablespoons butter
¼ cup chopped ham
1 egg

1 tablespoon minced parsley
1 teaspoon minced tarragon
Salt and pepper
1½ cups bread crumbs
Milk

STOCK

2 pounds beef shin, with meat
1 veal knuckle
2 carrots
2 turnips
2 leeks
Herb bouquet
2 teaspoons salt

SAUCE

2 cups stock
2 tablespoons butter
2 tablespoons flour
2 egg yolks
1 cup cream
Juice of 1 lemon

Remove wing tips, neck, and giblets from bird. Chop the liver. Cook onion in butter until wilted. Add to liver, along with ham, egg, seasonings, and crumbs that have been very slightly moistened with milk. Stuff chicken, sew up openings, and truss.

Put ingredients for stock in a large pot with 3 quarts of water. Add chicken wing tips, neck and giblets, and simmer for an hour, skimming several times. Lower the chicken into this broth (adding more water if necessary). Turn heat low and poach for 1½ hours, or until fork-tender. Remove to a platter and keep warm.

To make the sauce, strain off 2 cups of the broth. Thicken with a roux made with the butter and flour; beat egg yolks with cream and stir in slowly, beating vigorously with a French whip. Add lemon juice and correct seasoning. Arrange vegetables around chicken, if you wish, and serve with the sauce.

In the country, the soup and chicken are served at the same time. I prefer to enjoy the delectable soup, with the vegetables and soup meat cut up in it, at another time. I usually cook separate vegetables to serve with the chicken. Sometimes the stuffing is removed, sliced, and placed around the chicken when served.

★

## Chicken Raphael Weill

As a loyal San Franciscan and an old friend of the Weill family, I must include this famous dish, named for an outstanding and much-loved former citizen of the City by the Golden Gate. My understanding is that the dish was prepared by a chef of the noted Bohemian Club and served at a banquet in Mr. Weill's honor.

2 cloves garlic
1 cup (½ pound) butter
3-pound chicken, disjointed
Salt and pepper
1 jigger Cognac
½ cup chicken stock
½ cup dry white wine
Herb bouquet with tarragon
1½ cups cream
2 tablespoons sherry
Yolks of 3 eggs

Crush garlic and cook in butter until soft. Add chicken, sea-

[ 105 ]

soned with salt and pepper, and turn over gentle heat for 10 minutes, but do not brown. Pour Cognac over chicken, light, and when flames die down, add stock, wine and herbs. Cover and cook until tender. Remove to a serving dish. To the juices in the pan add cream, sherry, and salt and pepper to taste. Beat egg yolks slightly, add a little of the hot sauce, then whisk into remaining sauce. (This dish sometimes has mushrooms added, but they were not in the original recipe.)

★

## Chicken Roasted the French Way

Truss a tender roasting bird or capon. Strew over enough salt and pepper to season, and rub generously with little pieces of butter, pressing enough so the pieces adhere to the skin. Cook in a hot oven, 20 minutes to the pound, turning from time to time and basting frequently. When ready to serve, swizzle the bottom of the roasting pan with a little hot water, adding a little more butter if you think you should. Put this in the gravy boat. As simple as that, and so superior!

If you are French, you will serve at the same time a crisp green salad doused with French dressing, so you can mix the leaves of the lettuce in with the chicken sauce, as the French do. Try it.

★

## Roast Chicken with Tarragon

I once took a very small apartment in Nice, and the kitchen was the most minute one imaginable. The stove was ridiculous; it had two burners and an oven large enough to roast a wren. However, nothing daunted, I gave a lunch party, as there was a very pretty terrace and adequate space everywhere else but my *champ de bataille*. I decided to have this very excellent chicken, as it could be made in a roasting pan on top of the stove.

Choose 3 nice plump tender chickens. Salt and pepper the insides, and put inside, too, a generous egg of butter and a generous handful of tarragon. Truss the birds and brown in butter with 2 slices of onion and a large branch of tarragon. Put the birds in a roasting pan. Swizzle the skillet in which the chickens were browned with 1¼ cups of chicken bouillon, and pour over the waiting chicks. Cover and cook, either on top of the stove or in the oven, 40 minutes, basting and turning when necessary. During the cooking, pour over 2 glasses of dry white wine. Garnish the platter by surrounding the chickens with potatoes scooped into balls, partially boiled and browned in butter until cooked, and with button mushrooms stewed in butter. Serves eight.

★

### Poulet Sauté au Parmesan

This is exquisite!

> 3-pound chicken, disjointed
> Salt and pepper
> 3 tablespoons butter
> ½ cup grated Parmesan
> 1 cup sauce Mornay
> 2 tablespoons cracker crumbs

Sprinkle chicken with salt and pepper; sauté in the butter for 25 minutes, turning to color all sides. Sprinkle a little more than half the cheese on a flat baking dish, arrange the chicken on it, and cover with the sauce Mornay. Put in 350° oven for

5 minutes, sprinkle with remaining cheese and crumbs, and return to the oven until nicely browned and the chicken is tender. Serves three or four.

★

## Chicken Paprika with Sour Cream

> 4 small broiling chickens, split in halves
> Flour
> Salt and pepper
> ¼ pound butter
> 2 onions
> 2 cups sour cream
> 1 cup milk
> 3 tablespoons paprika

Dredge chicken halves with flour, season with salt and pepper, and sauté in butter, along with 1 of the onions, sliced thick. When nicely browned, remove onion, put chicken and second onion, cut in two, in a baking dish. Mix sour cream, milk, and paprika (which will make a good pink color) and salt to taste. Pour over chicken, cover, and bake in a 325° oven for half an hour or until the chicken is tender. Serves eight.

★

## Suprêmes of Chicken Violet Trefusis

So named because I was expecting this provocative lady for lunch, and I invented the dish in her honor.

> Breasts from 4 chickens
> Flour
> Salt and pepper
> Butter
> 1 small tin French mushrooms
> ½ pint cream

[ 108 ]

¼ cup Madeira
8 slices baked ham
1 small tin foie gras
1 small tin truffles

Separate the chicken breasts, dredge them in flour, sprinkle with salt and pepper, and brown lightly in ¼ cup of butter. Remove and keep warm. Drain the mushrooms and cook them in the same pan, adding more butter if necessary. When brown, sprinkle with a tablespoon of flour, add cream and Madeira, and correct seasoning. Simmer until the sauce is thickened and smooth. Butter a flat earthenware baking dish and arrange neatly trimmed ham slices on it. Cover each piece of ham with a chicken breast and put a slice of foie gras on each piece of chicken. Pour mushroom sauce over all and put in the oven until the chicken is tender and the sauce gilded. Just before sending in, lay a thin slice of truffle on each piece of chicken. Serves eight.

★

## Canard aux Navets (Duck with Turnips)

This is good French bourgeois cookery.

1 large duck
¼ cup (½ bar) butter
1 carrot
1 leek
1 onion
Herb bouquet
Salt and pepper
12 small peeled onions
24 small turnips (see Note)
Sugar
2 tablespoons flour

[ 109 ]

Brown duck in butter after removing wing tips. Meanwhile, to make stock, cover wing tips and giblets with 3 cups of water, add carrot, leek, and onion, cut in pieces, and the herb bouquet (a little rosemary in the bouquet is nice), and let simmer until needed. When the bird is golden, salt and pepper it, put it in a Dutch oven (or casserole), add the small onions, cover and cook gently for 45 minutes to 1 hour. Peel the turnips and cook them in some of the fat poured from the duck, for about 25 minutes, turning them so that they will brown on all sides. Sprinkle a teaspoon or so of sugar over them to glaze, and cook another 5 minutes. Remove duck and onions from casserole and pour off all but about 2 tablespoons of fat, add flour, and stir over heat until smooth. Strain the stock, which should now be reduced to 2 cups, into this roux, and cook, stirring, until thick and smooth. Correct seasoning, add turnips and carved duck. Serve with boiled or mashed potatoes and tender green beans.

★ NOTE: *The ducks in France are larger than the "ducklings" usually found here. A duckling is barely enough for four, yet the turnips will suffice for six or eight. I suggest that you use 2 ducklings. As for the turnips, 2 bunches are more than enough. They should be quartered unless very small. If they are cut in balls with a French cutter, allow 24 of them instead of the small turnips called for in the recipe.* H.E.B.

★

### Canard Rôti à l'Orange (Roast Duck with Oranges)

3 oranges
1 duck or duckling
Salt and pepper

2 jiggers (½ cup) Curaçao
1 cup veal or chicken stock
1 teaspoon glace de viande (or a bouillon cube)
2 tablespoons butter
2 tablespoons flour

Cut one orange in half and extract juice; reserve. Peel other oranges and slice ½ inch thick. Reserve good center slices, and put end pieces, cut up, inside the duck. Cover peel with water and simmer for 10 minutes, then drain and scrape off all white pith, leaving the zest, which should be cut into tiny slivers. Sprinkle duck with salt and pepper, and put in a 350° oven, breast down for the first 30 minutes. Roast for 1 to 1½ hours, depending upon the size of the bird. In a mortar pound the raw liver with half the orange zest; add the Curaçao. Heat the stock, add glace de viande, and thicken with the butter and flour kneaded together. Remove duck to a platter, surround with orange slices, and put in a low oven while you make sauce. Skim off all fat from the roasting pan, add orange juice, and stir to get all the brownings. Strain into liver mixture, add remaining orange slivers, and heat, adding salt and pepper to taste. If too thick, add a little water. Serves four.

★

### Partridge German Style

2 young partridge
Salt and pepper
2 diced carrots
2 diced onions
Herb bouquet
1 cup consommé
1 jigger (¼ cup) Cognac
1 cup sour cream

Clean and truss the birds, sprinkle with salt and pepper, and put in a Dutch oven or casserole with vegetables, herbs, and consommé. Bake in a 350° oven for 40 minutes, or until tender. Pour on Cognac, light, and when the flames die down, remove birds to a warm platter. Reduce liquid quickly, stir in sour cream, correct seasoning, and strain into a sauce boat. Serves four.

★

### Partridge Lucas

2 young partridge
Salt and pepper
¼ cup butter
12 small white onions
½ cup dry white wine
½ cup Madeira
½ cup consommé
2 dozen peeled chestnuts
Herb bouquet

Clean and truss the birds, season with salt and pepper, brown in butter, add peeled onions and brown slightly. Then add the liquids, chestnuts, and herb bouquet. Cover and cook in a moderate oven, basting frequently. When tender (30 to 60 minutes, depending upon age), arrange on a platter, surround with the vegetables, strain juices over all, and serve to four.

★

### Pheasant Braised with Cream

1 pheasant
3 thin slices salt pork
¼ cup butter
2 tablespoons chopped échalotes

1 jigger (¼ cup) Cognac
Salt and pepper
1 cup chicken stock
3 cups heavy cream
2 tablespoons wine vinegar
2 tablespoons grated horseradish

Clean and truss the bird, and bard by tying thin salt pork slices over the breast. Brown in butter, along with the échalotes. Add Cognac and flame. Sprinkle with salt and pepper, put in a casserole, rinse pan with stock and add; cover and cook in a 350° oven for 30 minutes, basting frequently. Add cream, vinegar, and horseradish, and bake another 10 to 20 minutes, or until tender. Correct seasoning and serve with rice and peas. Serves two to four, depending upon size of bird.

★

## Roast Pheasant

Stuff pheasant with special stuffing (page 132). Truss and bard with salt pork and sprinkle lightly with flour. Put in a roasting pan with 1 cup of Madeira and ½ cup of butter, and roast in a 375° oven, basting often, for about 30 minutes. Discard barding and continue roasting and basting for another 10 minutes, or until the juice runs clear when the bird is pierced. Do *not* overcook!

★

## Boned Braised Pigeons

This is from my grandmother's cookbook.

4 good-sized pigeons or squabs
¼ pound raw ham
¼ pound cooked tongue
¼ pound raw chicken breast

[ 113 ]

2 tablespoons chopped truffles
2 egg yolks
2 cups bread crumbs
Milk
2 teaspoons minced parsley
¼ teaspoon grated lemon rind
A little freshly grated nutmeg
½ teaspoon salt
Pepper
¼ cup butter
1 cup chicken broth

Have your meat man bone the squabs (a good butcher will do this). Make stuffing by grinding meats fine, adding truffles, egg yolks, bread crumbs moistened with milk, and remaining ingredients except butter and broth. Stuff and truss birds, arrange in roasting pan, and divide butter among them (1 tablespoon each). Add broth, cover, and bake in a 350° oven, basting with the broth, until tender — 45 to 60 minutes. Serves four. If served cold with a green salad, split birds carefully in two with a sharp cleaver or game shears. In this case they'll serve eight for luncheon.

★

## Pigeons or Squabs Marianne

8 small squabs or 4 large pigeons
1 cup olive oil
4 sliced échalotes
2 tablespoons minced parsley
2 tablespoons minced chives
1 teaspoon salt
Freshly ground pepper
16 thin slices bacon
1 thinly sliced lemon

½ cup water
½ cup white wine
¼ teaspoon glace de viande
1 egg yolk

If pigeons are used, have them split in half and gently flattened by the poulterer. Marinate in oil with seasonings and bacon for 3 hours. Put each on a papillote (parchment paper is ideal; foil may be used), divide bacon among them, fold paper, and fasten securely with a double fold and paper clips. Cook in a 350° oven for 20 minutes, turn and cook another 20 to 25 minutes, or until tender. Make a sauce by straining marinade, adding lemon slices, water, wine and meat glaze. Simmer 20 minutes; beat egg yolk with a little of the sauce, then beat into remainder. Heat gently, correct seasoning, and serve in a sauceboat with the birds. Serve the birds in their papers with the tops cut in an X with pointed scissors. Serves eight.

★

## Squabs with Grapes

8 squabs
Stuffing for squabs (page 131)
¼ cup butter
Salt and pepper
Paprika

SAUCE

2 pounds white grapes
¼ cup Cognac
1 cup consommé
2 tablespoons butter
Salt and pepper

Stuff and truss birds, spread with butter, sprinkle with salt, pepper and paprika, and roast in a 350° oven, basting frequently. This should take about 35 to 45 minutes. For the sauce, peel and seed the grapes. This process seems horrendous, but it is worth the trouble. It is a good plan to do it with a strong light nearby, as often one thinks the seeds are gone only to find another when the grape is held to the light. Combine with other ingredients, simmer 3 or 4 minutes, and serve poured around the squabs. Serves eight.

★ NOTE: *Bill Veach doesn't entirely approve, but seedless grapes can be used. The sauce may be thickened with a little beurre manié, too.* H.E.B.

★
## Quail Richelieu

2 quail
Salt and pepper
¼ cup butter
2 onions
2 celery ribs
2 turnips
2 carrots
1 cup consommé or chicken broth
1 tablespoon flour
1 truffle

Sprinkle quail with salt and pepper and brown on all sides in butter. Remove from pan. Cut vegetables julienne (in matchlike strips) and sauté in the same pan. Return birds to pan, add consommé, and cover pan. Simmer for 15 minutes or until tender. Put quail on a platter, surround with vegetables, and keep warm while you make a sauce. Mix the flour smooth with a little water. Add to the juices in the pan and cook, stirring, until well blended. Cut a truffle julienne, add to the sauce, correct seasoning, and serve with the birds. Serves two.

★

## Turkey in Champagne

We were to have a gala dinner, with guests at little tables of four, and the question was, what would be the pièce de résistance? Tracey Gaffey, a Los Angeles friend of mine, was in San Francisco with his attractive wife, Hazel, and as he is a chef of the first water, he suggested cooking a turkey in Champagne. I was fascinated with his recital, and also with his Irish enthusiasm. The only dark cloud on my horizon was that I had never deboned a turkey in my life, and it seemed too risky to try it out on a large party. He pooh-poohed this, saying that deboning a turkey was the easiest thing in the world and that he was very good at it. So, luckily, I agreed. Every single thing Tracey Gaffey said about this grand dish is true. And to bone a turkey is not a great bother. The thing is to get very sharp knives, with very sharp points. After once reaching the bone, you follow it closely. If it all seems too much trouble, the poultry man will do it for you.

When the bird is free of bones, cut the meat into cutlets that will make presentable helpings. Drop the pieces into a paper bag containing salt, pepper, and flour, and shake until the pieces are well coated. Then fry them, slowly, in plenty of butter, until they are golden in color. Now arrange the fried pieces in a deep casserole or roasting pan; pour over them the browned butter from the skillet, and also swizzle the pan with a little Champagne to capture all of the little bits and pieces. Then pour over ¾ bottle of Champagne. Cover dish and bake in a moderate (350°) oven for 45 minutes. If juices get low, put in the remainder of the bottle.

The party was a gay and merry one. George and Helen Cameron arrived with Elsa Maxwell, who had sent a case of

Mumm's to enliven the evening. Lily Pons was there with André Kostelanetz; the ever-lovely Mrs. Richard McCreery as sparkling as usual; Mrs. Robert Hays Smith in best form, later giving priceless imitations; Elsa played the piano, which she did extraordinarily well. These and the other guests all pronounced the turkey a masterpiece. So hooray for Mr. Gaffey!

★

## Turkey with Sauce Mornay

Slice enough cold turkey for four persons, preferably the breast, into uniform pieces. Lay the pieces in a well-buttered baking dish, the slices overlapping one another a little bit, making a parade down the center of the dish. Pour a cup of Mornay sauce all around the turkey. Slice ½ pound of mushrooms and sauté in 2 tablespoons of butter. Salt and pepper to taste. When done, lay these over the turkey, and then cover mushrooms with another cup of sauce. Sprinkle over the top 2 to 3 tablespoons of grated Parmesan cheese. Heat under the broiler until good and hot and gilded on top. Serve with boiled potatoes passed through a ricer. The dish warrants roasting a turkey expressly for making it. It is super for lunch.

★ NOTE: *If others are dark meat lovers, as we are, this is a wonderful way to use the breast.* H.E.B.

# SAUCES

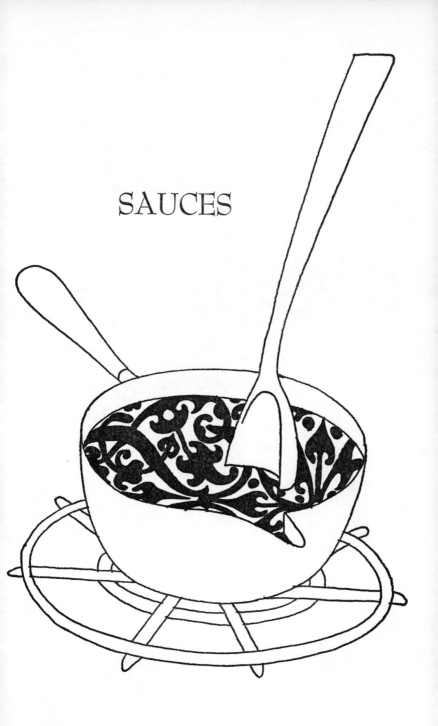

★
## Sauce Amandine

This recipe is from the Burlingame Country Club in California. They serve it on fillet of sole and other fish.

Brown ⅓ cup of blanched slivered almonds in 2 tablespoons of butter. Pour any surplus butter into a small saucepan, and to it add the juice of ½ lemon, ½ teaspoon of salt, a dash of cayenne, and 1 tablespoon of minced parsley. Heat, then add ¼ cup (½ bar) of butter, one slice at a time, beating it constantly with a whip. When all the butter has been added and the sauce is foamy, add the almonds and serve at once.

★
## Béarnaise Sauce

Reduce ¼ cup of vinegar containing 6 minced échalotes and a branch of tarragon (or ½ teaspoon dried tarragon) to half its volume. Pass through a sieve and cool. Put the vinegar, the yolks of 5 eggs, and ½ pound of butter in a double boiler and beat all the while it is warming. When butter has melted, and it is all incorporated into a sauce, finish by stirring in a tablespoon of finely minced tarragon and ½ tablespoon of minced chervil.

★
## Béchamel Sauce

¼ cup butter
¼ cup flour

1 pint chicken stock or milk or 1 cup
   each chicken stock and milk
Salt and pepper

Melt butter and stir in flour, making a roux. Stir over low heat for a minute or two to banish the raw taste of the flour. Add the liquid and beat smooth with a whip. Season to taste and simmer, stirring, until thickened. For a thin sauce, use only 2 tablespoons of flour. For a very thick sauce, increase it to 6 tablespoons.

★

## Caper Sauce

Make Béchamel sauce, using mutton broth for the liquid. Add ¼ cup of capers and 2 tablespoons of caper juice. If you prefer a richer sauce, add capers to hollandaise sauce.

★

## Cumberland Sauce

Squeeze an orange and a lemon, and marinate 1 teaspoon of finely minced échalotes in the juice. Simmer the orange peel in water for 10 minutes, scrape off all the white part or pith, and cut the zest into tiny slivers. Melt a glass of currant jelly, add a pinch of ginger, a dash of cayenne, ¼ teaspoon of salt, and ¼ teaspoon of grated orange rind. Heat with the juices and échalotes, then stir in the slivered rind. Serve hot or cold. This is usually served with game.

★

## Norma's Hollandaise

2 egg yolks
1 tablespoon lemon juice
1½ tablespoons water

¼ pound butter, cut in pieces
Salt

Have the egg yolks, liquids and butter cold. Put in top of double boiler. Stir constantly over boiling water until thick; season to taste with salt. Remove from heat at once. If too thick, add a tablespoon of cream.

★

## Mock Hollandaise

¼ pound butter, sliced
3 egg yolks
⅓ cup cold milk
1 teaspoon cornstarch
Juice of 1 lemon
Salt and pepper

Put all ingredients in top of double boiler and stir over boiling water until the butter melts and the sauce thickens. Be sure to stir constantly, and remove from heat as soon as thick.

★

## Sauce Madère

¼ cup chopped onion
4 slices bacon, diced
2 tablespoons butter
3 tablespoons flour
1½ cups bouillon
Herb bouquet
2 tablespoons glace de viande
¼ cup Madeira

Cook onion, bacon and butter together until onion is wilted. Add flour, stir smooth, then add bouillon and herb bouquet.

Simmer for 20 minutes; add glace de viande and Madeira. Heat and strain. Serve with game, sweetbreads, or veal.

★

## Sauce Mornay

Make Béchamel sauce, and add ½ cup of grated Parmesan, or enough to give it the cheese flavor you desire. If too thick, thin with a little milk or cream.

★

## Salsa con Chile

½ cup olive oil
2 minced cloves garlic
2 sliced onions
1 sliced green pepper
2 tablespoons tomato paste
1 tablespoon chili powder
Dash of Tabasco
½ teaspoon salt
2 cups water

Simmer all together for 20 minutes, then strain. This is to use with enchiladas or whenever a hot sauce is indicated.

★ NOTE: *A chile poblano, or Mexican green chile, may be used in place of the green pepper to make the sauce more authentic — and hotter!* H.E.B.

★

## Swedish Sauce

4 tart apples, peeled and sliced
1 cup white wine
1 cup grated horseradish
2 tablespoons mayonnaise

Cook apples in wine until soft and the wine evaporated. Pass through a sieve and mix with remaining ingredients. Cool. Serve with cold meats.

★

## Sauce Tomate

2 pounds firm ripe tomatoes
1 large onion, chopped
Herb bouquet
3 tablespoons butter
2 tablespoons flour
Bouillon
Salt and pepper
Sugar

Peel tomatoes and chop. Cook with onion and bouquet over a very low fire for ½ hour. Pass through a sieve. Make a roux with 2 tablespoons of butter and the flour, letting it brown a little. Add the tomato purée and simmer gently for an hour, adding a little bouillon if the sauce becomes too thick. Add a tablespoon of butter, salt and pepper to taste, and a few grains of sugar.

★

## Sauce Verte

Pick over a handful each of watercress, chervil, tarragon, and parsley. Cover with boiling water and let stand for 5 minutes. Drain, dry on a cloth to remove all moisture, chop and force through a sieve. Add to mayonnaise, along with a dash of prepared mustard. If sauce is not a handsome green, add a bit of green coloring. This sauce is delicious with cold boiled salmon or other cold fish.

★ NOTE: *If fresh tarragon and chervil are not available, half the amount of dried will have to be substituted. Soak it in hot water to soften. An easy way to make this sauce is to whirl it smooth in a blender.* H.E.B.

STUFFINGS

★

## Guatemalan Stuffing for Pork

Slice 2 medium onions and fry with 2 cloves of garlic in a little olive oil until brown. Remove the garlic and add 1 cup of ground beef, ½ cup of tomatoes, pepper and salt. Soak 1 cup of bread (with crusts removed) in a little milk, then press out milk and add bread to the mixture. Simmer half an hour, until the liquid from the tomatoes has been absorbed. Use this to stuff a boned shoulder, leg, or loin of pork, or double pork chops. I also like to first cook the pork in a casserole with consommé, then stuff it and reheat, basting with the consommé.

★

## Turkey Stuffing

This recipe is from Lee Eleanor Graham.

> 1 large loaf of bread
> ¼ teaspoon sage
> 2 teaspoons poultry seasoning
> ½ pound butter, melted
> 2 cloves garlic
> ½ cup chopped suet
> Salt and pepper

Crumble bread into crumbs. Add sage, which has been rubbed between the hands, and poultry seasoning, increasing or decreasing the amount to your taste. Add butter. Mince 1 clove of garlic and cook in the suet. Strain rendered fat into the bread mixture. Add another clove of garlic, minced or puréed, and salt and pepper to taste. This will be enough for a 10- to 12-pound turkey.

★

## Oyster Stuffing for Fowls

½ cup melted butter
1 cup soft bread crumbs
½ teaspoon freshly ground black pepper
1 tablespoon minced parsley
⅔ teaspoon salt
1 tablespoon lemon juice (or onion juice)
1½ dozen oysters, rolled in cracker crumbs, dipped into beaten
    egg, again in crumbs, and fried in ¼ cup of butter until
    golden

Pour the melted butter over the bread crumbs. Add the other ingredients and the oysters, and put inside your bird.

★ NOTE: *This is an interesting way of adding oysters to a dressing and, I think, preferable to the more usual way of chopping them. If you want more dressing, an extra cup of bread crumbs may be added because of the very generous amount of butter in the recipe.* H.E.B.

★

## Parsley Stuffing

1 large loaf white bread
2½ cups minced parsley
Thyme
Salt and pepper
½ cup melted butter

Remove crusts from bread and crumb. Add parsley, a slight trace of thyme, salt and pepper to taste, and the melted butter.

The stuffing should be light and not soggy with butter, and should spill off the spoon. The green color is very pretty, and the stuffing delicious.

## Turkey Stuffing with Chicken Livers

1 pound chicken livers
1 onion, minced
½ cup butter
¼ bay leaf
3 tablespoons minced parsley
⅛ teaspoon ginger
¼ pound (2 cups) bread crumbs
Salt and pepper
Milk

Cut livers in quarters and cook with onion in butter, until pink no longer shows. Crush the bay leaf in a mortar and add, along with other seasonings and bread crumbs. Mix, add just enough milk to moisten slightly, and season to taste. This is enough for a large chicken or small turkey.

★

## Stuffing for Ten Squabs

1 cup (about 4 ounces) chopped ham
½ pound large mushrooms
1 cup minced onion
3 tablespoons butter
1 cup minced parsley
4 cups soft bread crumbs
Salt and pepper

Cook the ham in its own fat for 3 or 4 minutes. Clean and slice the mushrooms thin. Cook them and the minced onion in the butter until they are soft. Combine with ham and other ingredients, adding a little more melted butter if too dry.

★ NOTE: *This is also an excellent stuffing for Cornish game hens, chickens, or pheasant.* H.E.B.

★

### Stuffing for Pheasant

    2 cups chopped cooked chestnuts
    2 or 3 minced truffles
    1 small tin foie gras or 2 small tins mousse de foie gras
    Salt and pepper to taste

Simply mix all ingredients and stuff pheasant.

★ NOTE: *This is a rich stuffing, and not exactly inexpensive, but when pheasants are served you're splurging anyway.* H.E.B.

# PASTAS, RICE
### and other
# FARINACEOUS DISHES

★

## Baking Powder Biscuits

2½ cups flour
2½ teaspoons baking powder
1 teaspoon salt
½ cup butter or lard
¾ cup milk

Mix flour, baking powder and salt. Work shortening in with your fingertips until the mixture is the consistency of meal. Add as much of the milk as is needed to make a firm dough. Roll out ¾ inch thick on a floured board, cut in small rounds, and bake in a 450° oven for 12 minutes, or until nicely browned. Makes about 24 small biscuits.

★

## Soft Corn Bread

This was a great favorite in my childhood.

1 cup white corn meal
1 tablespoon sugar
Salt to taste
1 tablespoon butter
2 cups milk
2 eggs
2 tablespoons flour
2 teaspoons baking powder

Put corn meal, sugar, salt, and butter in a bowl. Mix together and pour in boiling milk. Let stand 10 minutes. Beat eggs and flour together, add the baking powder, then mix with the corn meal mixture. Bake in an earthenware dish in a 400° oven for 20 to 30 minutes, or until set. Serves six.

★ NOTE: *This is more commonly known as spoon bread.* H.E.B.

★

## Sour Cream Hot Cakes

⅞ cup sifted flour
½ teaspoon salt
½ teaspoon soda
1 egg
2 tablespoons melted butter
1 cup sour cream

Sift dry ingredients together. Make a well in the center and pour in the slightly beaten egg, and the butter and sour cream. Mix well and quickly. Brush a hot griddle with oil. Drop large spoonfuls of batter upon it and cook the cakes until they bubble, then turn and cook other side. Serve at once on hot plates. This recipe will serve four gourmets, but only two gourmands!

★

## Foolproof Dumplings

This is Mrs. Constance Edwards's recipe.

1 cup flour (no need to sift)
1 heaping teaspoon baking powder
1 teaspoon salt
1 egg yolk
Milk

Blend dry ingredients with egg yolk, adding only sufficient milk to make a stiff dough, as the less milk, the drier will the dumplings be. Place, a teaspoon at a time, on top of stew, or fricassee of chicken or veal. Cover and cook 10 minutes without removing lid of saucepan. Will make about 12 dumplings.

★

## Homemade Fettucini

2 cups flour
1 teaspoon salt
2 eggs
3 tablespoons (about) cold milk

Sift flour with salt, add eggs, slightly beaten, and enough milk to make a very stiff dough. Cover and let stand in a cool (not cold) place for 2 hours. Roll *very thin* on a floured board and cut into narrow strips. Have on a table a towel. Lift up the strips with 2 forks and lay them carefully on the towel to dry. To cook, drop into plenty of salted boiling water and cook for about 10 minutes, or until just tender. Drain. Lift up with 2 forks while mixing in melted butter and grated Parmesan cheese. Also try mixing them with butter, then putting them in a casserole, covering the top with fine bread brumbs, and serving in place of potatoes.

★

## Fettucini alla Alfredo

Boil thin noodles, preferably freshly made, in salted water until just tender. Drain thoroughly and put in a heated bowl with warm melted butter, a little warm cream (which is the secret), and plenty of grated Parmesan cheese.

As you mix these together, do so with 2 forks, to keep the whole business nice and light, and keep the dish warm. At

[ 137 ]

Alfredo's, in Rome, it is done in a chafing dish, as the lifting up and down of the pasta chills it. As I say, the cream is the thing. Not too much, but just enough to make the butter and the cheese *onctueux*. Serve at once.

★

## Capelli di Angeli

The pasta used in this recipe is picturesquely known as angel's hair. It is the very finest variety and cooks very quickly.

> 2 cloves garlic
> ¼ cup olive oil
> 2 minced onions
> 2 minced green peppers
> 2 8-ounce tins tomato sauce
> Salt and pepper
> 2 pounds lean ground beef
> 1½ pounds capelli di angeli
> ¼ cup butter
> Grated Parmesan cheese

Slice garlic and cook in olive oil until it begins to color; discard garlic. Add onions and green peppers to oil, and when wilted add tomato sauce, and salt and pepper to taste. When the sauce bubbles, crumble the beef *on top* of the mixture. Do NOT STIR. Cook until *just* hot, but raw. In the meantime, cook the angel's hair in a large quantity of salted water. Drain, mix with butter, put in a large dish and pour sauce over it (or mix together, if you prefer). Serve with the cheese. Serves eight.

★

## Ravioli Florence Club

I record this for the elegance of the presentation — as a suggestion. The dough (see Homemade Fettucini, above) was rolled out to the last degree of thinness. Little demitasse spoonfuls of well-seasoned creamed spinach were uniformly spaced on a sheet of it, covered with a second sheet, and then cut with a small scalloped round about the size of a silver dollar. The rounds were cooked in boiling water and served with hot melted butter, from a pitcher, and freshly grated Parmesan cheese. No tomato sauce.

★

### Potato Gnocchi

2 pounds potatoes
2 eggs
2 egg yolks
¼ cup (½ bar) butter
1½ cups flour
2 teaspoons salt
Pepper and nutmeg

Peel potatoes and boil until tender. Force through a sieve or a ricer, add remaining ingredients and mix well, then form into little balls (using a rounded teaspoon for each, and lightly flouring the fingers). Flatten slightly with a fork, making a design with the tines. Have ready a large pot of boiling salted water, and drop the gnocchi into it. Cook a minute or two after they rise to the top, then remove with a slotted spoon. Serve with melted butter and grated Parmesan, or with sauce Espagnole. Makes about 80, enough for at least six persons.

★

### Semolina Gnocchi

1 cup semolina
Salt
Butter
Grated Parmesan cheese
3 beaten eggs

[ 139 ]

Cook semolina in 5 cups of water and 1½ teaspoons of salt until thick and smooth. Add 3 tablespoons of butter and ½ cup of cheese, remove from fire, and add eggs. Mix thoroughly and pour into a shallow pan; the mixture should be ½ inch thick. When cold, cut with a small round cutter and arrange on a well-buttered fireproof dish. Brush with melted butter, sprinkle with grated Parmesan cheese, and bake in a 350° oven for half an hour. Serves six.

★

## Macaroni with Mushrooms

1 pound fresh mushrooms
¼ cup butter
1 pound macaroni or spaghetti
Salt

Slice mushrooms and cook for 6 to 7 minutes in butter. Cook macaroni in boiling salted water. Drain and mix with the mushrooms. If you prefer, the mushrooms may be mixed with a cup of Béchamel sauce before adding to the macaroni. Serves six.

★

## Spaghetti Genovese

This is Mrs. George Washington Baker's recipe.

Boil spaghetti the usual way. (In Italy it is preferred *al dente* — still slightly resistant.) Drain well, then mix with the pungent aromatic sauce known as pesto (below). To serve, mix spaghetti and pesto together with the 2-fork motion described in the recipe for homemade fettucini. There should be enough of the sauce to give the spaghetti a pronounced greenish look. Have at hand a bowl of grated cheese.

I frequently made this dish for the ladies of the San Francisco Red Cross Motor Corps during the last World War. The head of the organization was my dear friend Mrs. Helen Cameron. It was a band of wonderful women, hard-working, daily putting in strenuous hours. I was made an honorary member of the group for this culinary contribution.

★

## Pesto

Remove coarse stems from parsley and fresh basil. Take 1 large handful of each and chop very fine. Put the herbs in a bowl, add 2 puréed cloves of garlic, and alternately add olive oil and grated Parmesan cheese until you have a sauce that is thick, yet runny (½ cup each is about right). Season with salt and pepper, cover and let stand for 24 hours. In the north of Italy, the pesto is further enhanced with the addition of finely chopped pine nuts.

★

## Rice Villa Sparta

This recipe is from Queen Helen, Queen Mother of Rumania.

> 1 cup rice
> 2 tablespoons mild olive oil
> Beef or mutton stock
> 4 large tomatoes
> Salt and pepper
> Tiny meat balls

Sauté rice in oil for 8 minutes over a low fire. Add stock to cover, and tomatoes which have been peeled, seeded, and cut in pieces. Season with salt and pepper, cover and cook until the liquid is absorbed and the rice is quite red. Correct seasoning, and serve with tiny meat balls. Serves four.

★ NOTE: *If liquid is absorbed before the rice is tender, add more.* H.E.B.

★

## Rice Pilaf

2 cups rice
2 onions, sliced
Butter
Consommé or chicken broth
Salt and pepper

Cook rice and onions in a large skillet with ¼ cup butter, turning them with a wooden spoon until they take color. Put in a casserole; add consommé or broth enough to cover rice by a finger's width. Cover and bake in a 350° oven for 17 minutes, then remove lid and stir *very gently* with a fork, just enough to disarrange the top layer of rice, which may have become hardened. Perhaps a little more cooking and a little more liquid will be needed — it depends upon the kind of rice used, also the shape of the pot. Rice must be dry and thoroughly done. Add another piece of butter. Serves four. Rice cooked this way using consommé Madrilène is a pleasing color. Or it may be cooked with a touch of saffron.

★

## Risotto with Truffles

1 onion, chopped
½ pound chopped beef
3 tablespoons butter (and more)
2 cups rice
Bouillon or beef stock
Grated Parmesan
1 cup truffles (see Note)
¼ cup Madeira
Salt and pepper

Cook onion and meat in 3 tablespoons of butter until the onion is wilted. Add rice and let it turn gold. Add bouillon enough to cover the rice by one-third its height, cover skillet, and cook slowly until tender and the liquid is absorbed. Add a good piece of butter (½ bar) and freshly grated Parmesan cheese, then the truffles, cut julienne and cooked for 3 or 4 minutes in the Madeira, and salt and pepper to taste. (A few spoons each of chicken broth and tomato sauce may also be added.) Serves eight.

★ NOTE: *Having just invested a sizable sum of money in a very few small cans of truffles, I wrote Bill Veach that a cup of them would cost a fortune. He did not deign to answer. I tested the recipe with a 4-ounce can of Urbani's puréed white truffles, and it was superb. As white truffles are Italian, I suspect that they are the kind the author intended.* H.E.B.

★
## Boston Baked Beans

3 cups white beans
½ pound fat salt pork
1 large onion, sliced
½ cup light molasses
1 teaspoon salt
1 tablespoon sugar
1 tablespoon dry mustard
½ cup boiling bean water

Soak the beans in water overnight. Next morning pick over and discard any blighted ones. Put the beans on to boil, having enough fresh water to cover them, and adding more when the beans expand. They are cooked when a bean splits its outside covering if blown upon. After that, do not overcook, but remove from the fire, drain, and save the bean water.

Cut salt pork into generous slices. Scald for several minutes in boiling water, and cut into pieces. Lay some in the bottom of a bean pot. Cover with half the beans and half the onion. Lay on more pork and follow with the rest of the beans, burying the other onion half in the beans. Put remaining pork on top of beans; pour over remaining ingredients, mixed together. Cover pot and bake in a slow oven for 6 hours, adding water as necessary if the beans dry out. Serves six or eight.

VEGETABLES

★
## Notes on Cooking Vegetables

There is absolutely no excuse for cooking vegetables over-time. They have then lost all nutritive value, and the flavor is also gone. Some say a vegetable is cooked when you can smell it, as for instance cauliflower; others say when the water begins to color, as with beans or asparagus.

One has to find a separate rule for each vegetable, arrived at by personal experience and observation. What is worse than stringy, tired asparagus tips, string beans cooked until gray, peas that have shriveled into bullets?

The veriest pinch of soda in water in which green vegetables are cooking will retain the color, and while there are some cooks who disdain this procedure, I am not interested in their hues and cries.

A pinch of sugar in tomatoes reduces their acid content and at the same time accents the flavor of the tomato itself.

In America, string beans cut into small slices are called "French cut," which is a misnomer, as one will never see beans cut so in France. Of course, the French have delicate little *mangetout* beans, which are very small, while we usually find in the market great outsized beans which have to be cut into edible size.

★ NOTE: *I can't allow the use of soda to go unchallenged, for the simple reason that the slightest bit too much will make the vegetables mushy. So if you must use it, use no more*

[ 147 ]

*than you can take up on a toothpick. Soda is also death on
vitamins, if you care.* H.E.B.

★

## Artichoke Bottoms with Cheese Soufflé

Artichoke bottoms (fonds) come in tins, and while not as
acceptable as fresh ones, they save much bother in preparation. This recipe may use either fresh ones that you have
cooked and trimmed neatly or canned ones.

> 12 artichoke bottoms
> 2 tablespoons butter
> ½ cup chicken or veal stock
> Cheese soufflé mixture (page 41)
> 2 tablespoons grated Parmesan

Heat the artichokes in the butter in a shallow baking dish
that is fireproof. Add the stock and simmer a minute, then dress
the center of each fond with a dome of the soufflé mixture.
Sprinkle with the grated cheese, moisten slightly with the liquid in the pan, and bake in a 350° oven until puffed and
golden. Serve with the pan juices, or with hollandaise mousseline sauce. Serves six.

★

## Asparagus

I prefer green asparagus, but there are some who prefer the
white variety as much as I do the green. The taste of each is
quite different, curiously enough.

Mrs. Lee Eleanor Graham, one of California's great hostesses, served both green and white asparagus on the same platter, in two different piles.

Choose about 10 handsome stalks per person. Cut off the

[ 148 ]

tough ends of the stalks, and try to have them all of even length. Take the most razor-edged kitchen knife you have and carefully remove the outer layer of skin, leaving the asparagus revealed in its greenness. Now arm yourself with a pair of kitchen tongs and have ready a large pot of boiling salted water. Drop in the asparagus, a few at a time so as not to reduce the water's heat. Let cook 9 to 12 minutes, according to the size of the stalks. If they are very thick, it may take a little longer, but *test*. The asparagus is done when a stalk, lifted up, has a slight tendency to bend. If the vegetable is to be served hot, drain at once and keep warm. If to be served cold, drop immediately into very cold water to arrest further cooking, then drain, cover with a cloth and put in a cool place, but beware of too long a time in the refrigerator, as the intense cold will tend to shrivel the beauties. Even when, at the last minute, they are placed in the refrigerator to chill thoroughly, cover them with cloth to prevent possible shriveling. This method is painstaking, but the beautiful jade green of the spears and the delight of the *convives* will more than compensate for the individual attention you have given to each single solitary spear.

★

## Beans (*Fagioli*)

Fagioli, in Italian, means beans, but in Tuscany it means especially a kind of white kidney bean known as "Romana"; it is worth hunting for them in an Italian market. They are boiled in salted water with an onion in it, until done; then the beans are drained, and served rather lukewarm. Accompanying the soup plate of beans are oil, vinegar, salt, pepper, and half a lemon. You doctor the beans with these condiments to your liking. Sometimes they are served with a sprinkling of minced parsley.

In Florence this dish is enhanced with, of all things, caviar! It is a truly Florentine *spécialité*. I find it somewhat so-so, and maybe I am shocked at the apparent waste of caviar. I only mention it as a gastronomic curiosity.

★

## Baked Cabbage

Shred a young tender cabbage and cook in boiling salted water for 4 minutes. Drain, put in a casserole, and dress with melted butter and salt and pepper to taste. Mix ½ cup of dried bread crumbs with 1 cup of cream and cover the top. Put in a 350° oven until very hot.

★

## Creamed Cabbage

The Comtesse Theobald de Vigneral, after cooking cabbage 15 minutes in boiling salted water, drains, chops, and mixes with a cream sauce (Béchamel). This is also very good. Be sure the cabbage is young and tender.

★

## Sweet and Sour Cabbage

1 quart shredded red cabbage
2 tart apples, peeled and sliced
2 tablespoons butter
1 cup water
2 tablespoons vinegar
¼ cup brown sugar
2 tablespoons flour
Salt and pepper

Put cabbage in a large skillet with apples and butter. Add water, cover and cook until apples and cabbage are tender, adding more water when necessary. Add vinegar, sugar, and flour, mixed together, and salt and pepper to taste. Simmer for 2 or 3 minutes and serve to four.

★

## Young Cabbage with Hollandaise

This recipe is from Mrs. John Magee, a New York, Newport, and Burlingame hostess.

Take *only* a very young cabbage. Divest it of its outer leaves. Quarter the cabbage and drop into boiling salted water for exactly 7 minutes, *and not a second longer!* Remove, drain, dry on a napkin, and keep warm, folded in the napkin, over hot water. Serve this masked with a sauce hollandaise. It will put a new complexion on the lowly chou.

★

## Carrots in Cream

This recipe is for the first tender young carrots of spring. Old ones simply will not do. If carrots are tiny, allow 8 or 10 for each serving.

Peel young new carrots. Put them in a saucepan with just enough water to cover. Add 2 cubes of sugar, a little salt, and ¼ cup of butter, and cook, covering the saucepan. When the carrots are tender and done, and the liquid well absorbed, pour in ½ cup of thick cream, and cook gently a little longer.

★ NOTE: *Although Bill Veach demands young carrots, more ancient ones, sliced very thin, are delicious cooked this way.* H.E.B.

★

## Cauliflower with Cream Sauce

Cook cauliflower flowerets in boiling salted water for 8 minutes, then drain and keep warm. Make the following sauce:

[ 151 ]

melt a tablespoon of butter in a double boiler, stirring into it a tablespoon of flour and a tablespoon of Grey Poupon Mustard. Blend this together, and then stir in ¾ cup of boiling water. Beat with a rotary egg beater, adding 2 egg yolks that have been thoroughly blended with a tablespoon or two of whipped cream. When well mixed, pour over the vegetable and serve.

★

## Cèpes Bordelaise

The cèpe is a large mushroom found in Europe in the late summer, September being the usual month for it to appear in the woods. It is practically unknown in cooking in America, but the taste is so delicious that I counsel the uninitiated to try a tin of these fungi. They are procurable in large cities at the best food shops.

Cèpes should be freshly picked when used. Cut off the bottom of the stem, wash the mushrooms in cold water, dry, then slice. If you are using tinned cèpes, drain off all their liquid as well as possible, and then slice. From then on, the procedure is the same for either the fresh or tinned variety. Drop the cèpes in hot olive oil and cook 5 minutes. Then add some finely chopped échalotes, salt, pepper, a crushed clove of garlic, and a heaping tablespoon of minced parsley. Let cook, slowly, until the fresh cèpes are thoroughly softened, or the tinned cèpes have a nice brown color. Before serving, give them a squeeze of lemon juice. A peeled seeded tomato will also enhance these mushrooms.

The tinned cèpes are expensive, but when they accompany a beautiful tender sizzling beefsteak, they will justify any extravagance.

★

## To Boil Corn

Use very freshly picked corn and do not remove the husks until you are ready to cook it. Then drop into boiling salted half water, half milk, and cook only 5 or 6 minutes, according to the size of the ears. If the corn is to be served at a large open-air luncheon, as frequently happens at Rosecourt, the Burlingame house of Mrs. George Cameron, it is left in the liquid, which has been somewhat cooled, and kept on the corner of the outdoor range, where the corn will stay warm but will not cook any longer. The milk tends to tenderize the corn, but the short cooking is the real secret. Serve with plenty of sweet butter and salt and pepper.

★

## Corn Fritters: Two Methods

(1). Prepare 2 cups of grated fresh tender young corn (6 large ears). Stir in 3 beaten egg yolks. Add 1 teaspoon of salt, ¼ teaspoon of freshly ground pepper, 1 teaspoon of sugar, and fold in the whites of the 3 eggs, stiffly beaten. Cook on a buttered griddle by the tablespoonful. Turn once.

(2). Grate 6 to 8 ears of corn. Season with salt, pepper and some paprika. Beat 1 egg very light and stir into corn, along with 1 tablespoon of melted butter, ½ cup of milk, and 2 tablespoons of flour (or enough to hold all together). Drop by large spoonfuls in a generous quantity of hot butter, frying to a golden brown. Drain and serve. Both recipes serve six.

★

## Corn in the Javanese Manner

This will add spice to the conversation at table.

Cut fresh corn from the cob with a very sharp knife. Season

[ 153 ]

with salt and pepper, and cook in a little cream until done —
only a few minutes. Put the corn in a buttered baking dish,
cover with a layer of freshly grated coconut, and brown in the
oven. Use your own good sense about proportions, going on
the assumption that 1½ ears of corn will just about suffice for
one serving.

★

## Corn Timbale

1 No. 2 can cream-style corn
6 eggs
1 teaspoon paprika
Salt, pepper, and cayenne
1 tablespoon minced parsley
1 pint whipping cream
Butter

Whirl corn in the blender or force through a food mill. Beat
eggs until light, add seasoning, and blend with the corn. Fold
in the whipped cream. Put in a buttered ring mold, set the
mold in a bain-marie, and bake in a moderate oven (350°)
about 20 to 25 minutes, or until the custard has set (test by
inserting a knife). Do not let the water in the bain-marie boil.
When done, turn out of mold, and serve with the center filled
with creamed chicken or crab, or shrimps and Olympia oysters.
Or — for a less stylish dish — with old-fashioned stewed tomatoes.

★

## Eggplant with Anchovies

This recipe is from Provence.

1 eggplant
Olive oil

1 small tin anchovies
3 cloves garlic
Bread crumbs
3 tablespoons strong beef bouillon
Freshly ground pepper
Minced parsley

Cut eggplant in half lengthwise. Score the flesh ½ inch deep in a crisscross pattern. Sauté flesh side down in ¼ cup of olive oil. Put in a baking dish, cut side up. Mash the anchovies and the garlic to a paste, using a mortar and pestle. Add ¼ cup bread crumbs, which have been soaked in the bouillon, and plenty of freshly ground pepper. Blend very well and spread over the top of the eggplant. Sprinkle with minced parsley and a few more bread crumbs, then spoon a little olive oil over all. Bake in a 400° oven for ½ hour. Serves four to six, depending upon size of eggplant.

★

## Curried Eggplant

1 eggplant
Butter
1 pound cooked prawns (jumbo shrimps)
1 cup coconut milk (see Note)
1 clove garlic, sliced
2 large onions, sliced
2 teaspoons curry powder
½ teaspoon ginger
1 tablespoon vinegar
1 tablespoon water
Salt

Peel eggplant and cut in cubes. Cook in ¼ cup of butter until lightly browned. Add shelled and cleaned prawns and coconut milk. In another pan, brown the garlic and onions in another ¼ cup of butter. Add curry powder, ginger, vinegar and water. Cook slowly for 7 minutes, and combine with eggplant mixture. Cook slowly until eggplant is tender, add salt to taste, and serve with rice and condiments.

★ NOTE: *Coconut milk is easily made by grating a coconut and covering with boiling water. Let stand an hour, then strain through a heavy cloth, wringing out all liquid.* H.E.B.

★

## Fried Eggplant

Cut eggplant early in the morning in ½- to ¾-inch slices, and sprinkle with salt. Cover with a weight and let stand several hours, then wipe the slices free of salt and pour off the liquid that has accumulated. Beat an egg and season well, but be sparing with the salt. Dip eggplant slices in fine cracker crumbs, in the egg, and again in the crumbs, and fry, in a basket, in boiling lard. Eggplant is very absorbent. If it is not prepared beforehand in such a way as to resist the grease in which it is cooked, the result will be soggy with fat, and quite disgustingly indigestible.

★

## Eggplant Soufflé

1 large eggplant
¼ cup butter
Thick Béchamel sauce
3 tablespoons grated Parmesan cheese
2 eggs, separated
Salt and pepper

Cut the eggplant in half lengthwise, and cook, cut side down, in the butter. When soft, carefully scoop out the insides, leaving not too thin a shell. Mash insides well, measure and mix with an equal amount of thick Béchamel sauce, the cheese, and the egg yolks, well beaten. Add salt and pepper to taste, beat the egg whites until stiff, and fold in. Fill eggplant shells and bake in a 350° oven for 30 to 35 minutes, or until risen and brown. Serves four to six.

★ NOTE: *If the eggplant is a large one, add another egg.* H.E.B.

★

## Eggplant Toulouse

1 eggplant
Salt
Flour
½ cup olive oil
1 large clove garlic
3 tablespoons minced parsley
3 cups small dice of bread

Slice eggplant the long way and quite thin, as they do in Gers, France. Sprinkle with salt and let stand 2 hours, then drain, dry, and dip in flour. Cook in plenty of olive oil until brown and almost crisp. Remove from pan and drain on paper toweling. Keep warm. Peel the garlic and crush slightly, then put in the same olive oil, along with the parsley. When hot, add the bread and cook, stirring, until brown and crisp. Sprinkle over the eggplant slices, and serve very hot. Serves six.

★

## Ratatouille

This is a dish from Provence.

1 eggplant
4 large tomatoes

2 large onions
2 cloves garlic
2 green peppers
2 sweet red peppers
½ cup olive oil
Salt and pepper
2 zucchini (optional)

Peel and slice eggplant; peel tomatoes, divest of seeds, and slice; slice onions and garlic thin; slice zucchini; slice peppers into large slivers, discarding pith, stems, and seeds. Oil a baking dish. Lay the vegetables in, one kind at a time, then repeat, salting and peppering lightly as you go along. When dish is full, pour over all the oil, little by little. Cover the casserole and bake 45 minutes in a moderate oven. Serves six. Excellent hot, and also cold as an hors d'oeuvre.

★

## Flageolets

These delicious beans are almost unknown in the United States, but they are procurable canned in the specialty food shops. They faintly resemble, in color, the Lima bean, a legume almost equally unknown in France. If you want to experiment with them, and I hope you will like them as I do, open a tin, drain, and put the beans, with a little of their liquor, in a casserole to heat. Also cut 2 or 3 slices of thick bacon into small squares and fry, but not too crisp. When the beans are hot, add the bacon with a little of the grease. This is an excellent winter dish.

★

## Mushrooms in Cream

2 pounds mushrooms
¼ pound butter

2 tablespoons minced parsley
1 tablespoon flour
1 teaspoon sugar
3 eggs
1 cup cream
Salt and pepper

Wash and slice the mushrooms, discarding gritty stem ends. Cook over a low flame with the butter, parsley, flour, and sugar, until the juices have almost evaporated. Mix eggs, slightly beaten, with cream, and add to mixture, cooking over low heat until thickened. Season with salt and pepper, and serve over fried bread or, better still, in a vol-au-vent case. Serves six to eight.

★

## Mushrooms and Parmesan Cheese

2 pounds mushrooms
¼ cup (½ bar) butter
Salt, pepper, and paprika
2 tablespoons bouillon
2 tablespoons grated Parmesan cheese

Wash and slice mushrooms, and stew them gently in the butter for about 20 minutes; during the cooking add salt, pepper, and paprika to taste. Add bouillon and cheese, mix well, and serve at once. Serves six to eight.

★

## Mushroom Pie

Pastry for a 2-crust pie
2 pounds mushrooms
¼ pound butter
1 tablespoon minced onion

1 cup Béchamel sauce, made with cream
Salt and pepper

Line an 8-inch pie pan with pastry. Wash and slice mushrooms and cook in butter with the onion for 10 minutes. Add Béchamel and salt and pepper. Cool, then fill pastry shell, and cover top with strips of pastry in lattice fashion. Bake in a 400° oven until nicely browned, approximately 25 to 30 minutes. Serves six to eight.

★

## Mushroom Soufflé

1 pound fresh mushrooms
Butter
1 cup rich milk
⅛ cup flour
1 cup cream
Salt and pepper
4 eggs, separated

If you are lucky, you'll have nice pink mushrooms, picked from the fields. Wash and slice, then stew in 2 tablespoons of butter for 8 to 10 minutes. Add milk, simmer 15 minutes, then strain out mushrooms and reserve. Make a roux with ⅛ cup of flour and ⅛ cup of butter, add the mushroom milk, cream, and salt and pepper to taste. Cook until thick and smooth, then add egg yolks, well beaten; mix well and cool. Beat egg whites until stiff, fold into mixture, pour into a buttered mold, place in a bain-marie, and bake in a 425° oven for 20 minutes, or until soufflé mounts. Reheat reserved mushrooms and serve with soufflé. Serves four to six.

★ NOTE: *If you prefer, and I do, mix the mushrooms with the soufflé before folding in the egg whites.* H.E.B.

★
## Fried Parsley

Fried parsley is rarely encountered nowadays. It is a pity, as it makes a beautiful garnish, and is good to boot. The best variety of parsley to use is the springy curly kind. Italian parsley, despite its excellent flavor, is not so satisfactory. Wash the parsley thoroughly and dry it even more scrupulously. Any water left on the herb will spoil the frying, so not one drop, please! Put the parsley into a basket and drop into very hot (380°) fat. Be very careful, as the grease will spatter. Also take great care, as the parsley will be done at once! *It cooks immediately.* One second too long and it will lose its green and be horrid.

★
## On Cooking Peas

When one is so fortunate as to have a kitchen garden, one of the greatest delights is to have lovely, tiny, succulent peas picked fresh in the morning for lunch that very day. These should be dropped into boiling, slightly salted water, to which a few of the tender pods have been added, and allowed to cook for a bare 5 minutes. Season, after draining and removing pods, with a generous piece of fresh butter. If you have only slightly salted the water, save the liquid for the soup pot.

However, for bigger, older peas, that have passed their first stage of lusciousness, the old French method, devised with the usual Gallic culinary ingenuity, is best. Put them in a pot with ½ head of lettuce, an onion, a carrot, and a cube of sugar (or 2, depending upon quantity). Add a tablespoon of water, cover closely, and cook slowly in the liquid that accrues from the vegetables. Before serving, remove onion, carrot and lettuce, and add an egg of butter.

[ 161 ]

My Italian cook's method is somewhat different. In with the peas he puts parsley, an onion, salt, pepper, and a little olive oil along with a tiny bit of water. The butter goes in after the peas are cooked. The pot is covered during the cooking. I must say they are good.

★

## Stuffed Peppers

Select 6 beautiful sweet red or green peppers of uniform size. Remove a slice from the top (or cut lengthwise) and discard stem and seeds. Make a panada with 3 cups of bread crumbs mixed with just enough hot rich milk — about ½ cup — to make a thick paste. Add 1½ cups of ricotta or cottage cheese and salt and pepper to taste, then stir in ½ to ¾ cup of diced Gorgonzola cheese. Stuff peppers with the mixture and put in a baking dish brushed with olive oil. Bake in a 350° oven for 30 minutes, basting a few times with olive oil. Serves six.

★

## Potatoes Anna (Pommes Anna)

6 cups sliced potatoes
½ cup butter (or more)
Salt and pepper

Peel and cut potatoes in uniform slices, and soak in cold water. Butter a flat-bottomed baking dish about 3 inches high, and line bottom and sides with paper cut to fit. Butter paper well, and arrange a layer of potatoes on the bottom in a symmetrical manner, each slice slightly overlapping the next one. Sprinkle with salt and pepper, and cover with a tablespoon of butter. Repeat until the potatoes are used. Cover dish and bake on bottom shelf of a 400° oven for an hour, or until the potatoes are tender, basting several times with more melted butter.

[ 162 ]

Drain off butter, turn upside down on a platter (careful!), and remove paper. The bottom and sides should be beautifully brown.

★

## Pommes Château

Peel potatoes of uniform size; parboil in water or bouillon. Drain, roll in melted butter, and bake in a 375° oven until tender and brown.

★

## Potato Barquettes

Add 1 slightly beaten egg to 2 cups of well-seasoned mashed potatoes. Form into little boats or cups, brush with melted butter, put on a buttered cookie sheet, and bake in a 375° oven until brown. Fill with peas and use as a garnish for a roast.

★

## Potato Croquettes

2 cups cold mashed potatoes
½ teaspoon salt
¼ teaspoon celery salt
⅛ teaspoon pepper
2 tablespoons butter
1 egg yolk
1 teaspoon minced parsley
½ teaspoon grated onion
1 egg
Crumbs

Mix all together except last two ingredients; chill and form into croquettes. Dip in egg, then crumbs, and fry in deep fat at 375° until nicely browned. Serves four.

★
## Mashed Potato Casserole

3 cups mashed potatoes
2 tablespoons melted butter
1 cup cream
Salt and pepper
2 eggs, separated

Mix potatoes, butter, cream, and salt and pepper to taste. Beat egg yolks, mix in well, then beat whites stiff and fold in. Pile in a buttered 1-quart casserole, and bake in a 375° oven until hot and brown. Serves six.

★
## Gratin de Pommes à la Dauphinoise

In the country where this dish originates, grated Gruyère is used, but I prefer Parmesan.

5 potatoes
Butter
Salt and pepper
1 cup grated Gruyère or Parmesan cheese
2 cups milk
1 egg

Peel and slice potatoes, and arrange in layers in a well-buttered baking dish, sprinkling each layer with salt, pepper, and cheese. Have cheese on top. Mix egg and milk and pour over all. Dot with butter and bake in a 350° oven for 45 minutes, or until the potatoes are tender. Serves six.

★
## Pommes Duchesse

2 pounds potatoes
Butter

[ 164 ]

2 eggs
2 egg yolks
Salt and pepper

Peel and boil potatoes, then force through a sieve or ricer. Mix with 2 tablespoons of butter, eggs and egg yolks beaten together, salt and pepper to taste. Force through a pastry bag in small rosettes onto a buttered cookie sheet, or form in balls. Paint with melted butter and bake in a 425° oven until nicely browned. Serves six.

★

## Pommes Florentine

2 pounds sliced potatoes
1 cup grated Parmesan cheese
2 tablespoons flour
Salt and pepper
Butter
Consommé or bouillon

Mix ¼ cup of the cheese and the flour together, and dredge the potatoes with it. Butter a baking dish and arrange potatoes in layers, sprinkling each layer with cheese, a little salt and pepper, and tiny peas of butter. Have cheese on top, and pour over enough bouillon to barely come to the top. Bake in a 350° oven for an hour, or until the liquid is absorbed. Serves six.

★

## Potatoes Hashed in Cream

4 boiled potatoes
1 minced onion
2 tablespoons butter
Salt and pepper
½ cup cream

Cut potatoes in small dice. Sauté the onion in the butter, add potatoes and mix well. Season with salt and pepper. Allow to cook brown on the bottom, then pour in cream and stew gently until the potatoes are tender. Finish in a 400° oven just long enough to brown the top. Serves four.

★

### Potatoes au Gratin

6 potatoes
2 chopped onions
Butter
2 tablespoons flour
½ cup bouillon
2 cups cream
Salt and pepper
1 teaspoon minced parsley
Grated Parmesan cheese
Bread crumbs

Steam potatoes until just tender; peel and slice. Cook onions in 2 tablespoons of butter until golden; add flour, bouillon, cream, salt and pepper to taste, and cook until smooth and thickened. Stir in parsley. Butter a baking dish and arrange potato slices in layers. Cover each layer with sauce and sprinkle with cheese. Have top layer sauce, then cheese, crumbs, and peas of butter. Bake 25 minutes in a 350° oven. Serves six.

★

### Pommes Lorette

1 cup milk
¼ tablespoon butter
½ teaspoon salt

1 cup flour
4 eggs
2 cups Duchesse potatoes
Deep fat for frying

Bring milk to a boil, add butter and salt. When butter has melted, put in flour all at once, and stir over heat until it forms a ball in the pan. Beat in the eggs, one by one. Combine with Duchesse potatoes. Drop by teaspoons into deep fat (370°) until puffed and brown. Drain on paper napkins. Serves eight.

★

## Pommes Macaire

6 baked potatoes
Butter
Salt and pepper

Scoop out insides of freshly baked potatoes and mash smooth. Add 3 tablespoons of butter, salt and pepper to taste. Melt ¼ cup of butter in a skillet, add potatoes and press them down evenly, using a pancake turner. When nicely browned on the bottom, turn — it should turn in one piece — and brown the other side, slipping a little more butter underneath, if necessary. Serve like a pie, cut in wedges. Serves six.

★

## Potato Pancakes

2 cups grated raw potatoes
2 eggs
½ cup milk
1 cup flour
3 teaspoons baking powder
1 teaspoon salt
4 tablespoons melted butter

Drain the potatoes after grating. Beat the eggs and add to the potatoes; add milk and other ingredients and stir well. Fry, by the tablespoonful, on a greased griddle.

★

## Purée de Pommes à la Ali Bab

This is a recipe from Ali Bab's famous cookbook. In his opinion it is "the best recipe."

Peel a pound of potatoes, sprinkle with salt, and steam until tender, then pass through a ricer. Mix in a pound of very fresh butter and a little more salt. Serves three, according to Ali Bab.

★ NOTE: *I tried this and the result was thickish melted butter. I checked Ali Bab's recipe and the above, as given, is correct. I wrote Bill Veach and he replied, "I have tried this recipe and it is superb." That put me on the spot. I asked Jim Beard and he said the butter had to be added piece by piece, and cold. So I tried that. The result wasn't quite as runny, but it was cold. I include the recipe only for the laugh it will give you. H.E.B.*

★

## Pommes Rouennaise

Peel potatoes of uniform size. Put them in boiling water and cook until they are *nearly* done, for they must not be mushy or ready to fall apart. Let the potatoes get cold. Then, to serve, drop them into a saucepan of boiling fat, removing when they're golden and crusty on the outside. Drain on absorbent paper. You will find the interior of the spuds delightfully luscious and "fondant" when cooked this way.

## Pumpkin au Gratin

If this is served on toast, it is like a digestible and delicious Welsh Rabbit.

2 pounds pumpkin
1 cup water
½ teaspoon salt
2 cups thick sauce Mornay
2 tablespoons each grated Gruyère and Parmesan cheese
1 tablespoon butter

Peel pumpkin, discard seeds, and cut in pieces. Put in a heavy pot with water and salt, cover and cook until tender — about 1 hour — stirring occasionally. Put through a sieve or food mill, mixing with the sauce Mornay. Correct seasoning and put in a buttered casserole. Sprinkle with cheese, dot with butter, and brown in a 350° or 400° oven. Serves six.

★ NOTE: *There is no reason why Hubbard or banana squash can't be used for this — nor canned pumpkin, for that matter. In the latter case, use a No. 2½ can.* H.E.B.

★

## Spinach Gnocchi

This appetizing dish is of Italian origin.

2 pounds spinach
1 pound ricotta cheese
1 cup grated Parmesan cheese
1 egg
2 tablespoons flour
1 cup soft bread crumbs
1 teaspoon salt (or more)
Pepper and nutmeg
Melted butter

[ 169 ]

Cook the spinach in a minimum of water, drain, and squeeze out *all* water. Chop. Mix in the ricotta cheese, ¼ cup of Parmesan, egg, flour, crumbs, salt, pepper, and a good bit of freshly grated nutmeg. Taste and add more salt if necessary. Take the mixture up by the teaspoonful and form into shapes the size of your little finger (dusting your hands with flour helps). Roll gnocchi in flour, and drop a few at a time into simmering salted water. Let cook a minute after they rise to the surface, then lift out with a slotted spoon. Pour melted butter over them, sprinkle with remaining cheese, and serve very hot. Serves eight.

★ NOTE: *This is very much like malfatti, a dish supposedly resulting from a badly made batch of ravioli. It is marvelous, nevertheless.* H.E.B.

★

## Tomatoes Stuffed with Cheese

6 large firm tomatoes
¼ cup finely minced échalotes
Butter
1 cup bread crumbs
¼ cup minced parsley
¼ cup grated Swiss cheese
¼ cup grated Parmesan cheese
Salt and pepper

Cut tomatoes in halves horizontally; gently squeeze out seeds and carefully scoop out a little. Place tomato halves in a shallow baking dish. Cook the shallots in ¼ cup of butter until soft, and add remaining ingredients with salt and pepper to taste. Stuff tomatoes, brush each with melted butter, and bake in a 350° oven for 25 minutes, or until brown and tender, but not falling apart. Serves six.

★
## Tomatoes Creole

2 tablespoons butter
1 large onion, finely chopped
1 medium-sized green pepper, cored, seeded, and minced
1 large tin tomatoes or 6 large ripe tomatoes, peeled, seeded, and chopped
2 tablespoons sugar
Salt, pepper and bay leaf

Put butter in skillet. Add onion and pepper. When softened, add the tomatoes, sugar, salt to taste, pepper ditto from a mill, and a bay leaf. Simmer a long time very slowly; must be dark and thick.

★
## Tomato Soufflé with Tarragon

The tomato-tarragon combination is indeed a happy one.

4 pounds ripe tomatoes
2 cups thick cold Béchamel sauce
6 eggs, separated
Salt, pepper, and nutmeg
2 tablespoons fresh tarragon, minced

Peel and seed tomatoes, and cook until very thick in a heavy pan over low heat. Force through a sieve or food mill; you should have 2 cups of purée. Mix with the Béchamel sauce and egg yolks, well beaten. Season to taste with salt, pepper, and nutmeg, and add tarragon. Beat egg whites stiff and fold in. Pour into a buttered 1½- or 2-quart soufflé dish, and bake in a 350° oven until well risen and brown. Serves six to eight.

★
## Tomatoes Stuffed with Scrambled Eggs

Peel 8 medium-sized ripe but firm tomatoes. Cut off stem ends a very little, to enable the tomatoes to stand up well; remove all core, extract the seeds, and leave inside empty for the scrambled eggs to come. You must be sure that the tomato shells remain firm. Scramble 10 eggs in a double boiler, using ¼ cup of cream. Season with salt and pepper, and do not overcook the eggs. Carefully fill the tomatoes with the scrambled egg mixture, putting each one, cut end down, on a flat baking dish. Put into a 400° oven for 5 minutes or until tomatoes are thoroughly heated. Have ready 1 cup of sauce Mornay. To serve, remove the tomatoes with great care to a serving platter, and surround with the sauce, so you have red islands swimming in a sea of sauce. Sprinkle over each tomato a grain of sugar, salt, and white pepper. Serves eight. Sauce hollandaise mousseline is also delicious with this dish.

★
## Turnips

Turnips are more interesting if they are boiled in salted water, then scooped out and filled with spinach or peas, to surround a dish. If you are fortunate enough to find young tiny baby turnips, which you peel and boil in salted water just long enough to be tender and still hold their sweetness, pour over them a little melted butter and you will have a real treat. Baby turnips boiled this way and then braised in butter, with a little sugar to give them color, are also a true delicacy.

SALADS
and
SALAD
DRESSINGS

★

## Green Salad

Far and away the best salad of all is composed of succulent lettuce leaves, washed, dried, wrapped in a towel to crisp in the refrigerator, and dressed with French dressing, with the possible addition of minced chives, chervil, and tarragon (fines herbes). I have become allergic to the term "tossed salad." In France one notes that salads are treated gently, lightly turned with a fork and spoon so that all the leaves will be bathed in dressing, but without bruising. This simple salad is a perfect accompaniment to any meal.

★

## Artichoke Salad

Cook artichokes, remove chokes and tough leaves that surround the chokes, and replace with scooped-out lemon halves filled with mayonnaise.

★

## Asparagus and String Bean Salad

Remove tough ends of white asparagus (if not available, use green), and cook until just tender. Cook young string beans until just tender. Combine and sprinkle with thinly sliced truffles. Marinate in French dressing for 30 minutes.

[ 175 ]

★
## Bird's Nest Salad

This is my one and only contribution to "pictorial" salads, but it is not bad, and is amusing to look at.

Select young chicory lettuce (curly endive) heads — one for each person to be served. Trim off all the outside leaves, and cut the stem in such a way that you leave the center leaves intact. This is your "nest." On each nest lay a few lichees (which come in tins from China) — drain the fruit of its juice, and place in the center of each nest. These are your "eggs." Pour over a tart French dressing mixed with a very little mayonnaise.

★
## Cabbage Salad

Take off the outside leaves of a very fresh young cabbage. Remove the stem, then slice the head paper-thin with the very sharpest of knives. Cover it with the following dressing: 1 tablespoon of lemon juice, 3 tablespoons of olive oil, 1 tablespoon of cream, and salt and pepper from the mill to season. If you need more dressing, double the amount, using the same proportions. Let the cabbage marinate in the dressing for an hour before serving. It is excellent.

★
## Caviar Ring

This recipe was given me by the late Mrs. Robert Dunham, a famous hostess in San Francisco and Chicago.

1 envelope plain gelatine
½ cup cream
1 cup caviar

[ 176 ]

 1 cup cream, whipped
 1 cup highly seasoned mayonnaise

Cover gelatine with the cream and let stand 10 minutes, then put over hot water to dissolve. Mix caviar, whipped cream, mayonnaise, and gelatine together and pour into a 2-quart ring mold. Let it stand for 4 hours in the refrigerator. Unmold and fill center with avocado, cover with French dressing, then top with shrimps or crab. Put lovely little lettuce leaves around the edge. Serves six.

★ NOTE: *A cup of caviar is ½ pound, which will cost considerable. When I protested, Bill Veach said: "Use red caviar if you are not in a spendthrift mood." I think I'd rather use pressed caviar or cut the quantity in half.* H.E.B.

★

## Chicory and Apple Salad

Mix chicory (curly endive) and sliced apples together, with a generous sprinkling of grated Gruyère cheese. Dress with a sauce vinaigrette, seasoned with a very little Savora or Maggi.

★

## Cucumber and Cheese Ring

 1 pound cottage cheese
 1 cup sour cream
 1 cup mayonnaise
 2 tablespoons grated onion
 2 envelopes plain gelatine
 ½ cup milk
 2 long, thin cucumbers
 Salt and pepper
 12 cherry tomatoes, sliced
 2 thinly sliced Spanish onions

[ 177 ]

Sieve cottage cheese, mix with sour cream, mayonnaise, and onion. Soften gelatine in milk, dissolve over hot water, and add. Peel and seed cucumbers, discard seeds, cut in tiny dice, and stir into mixture. Season to taste with salt and pepper and pour into a charlotte mold or deep cake pan. Chill, unmold, and decorate top, around the edge, with tomatoes, the slices overlapping. Put onion rings, which have been soaked in salted ice water, around the base. Serves six to eight.

★

## Egg Salad

Constance, a French cook I once had, made an exceptional salad through misunderstanding my instructions. I had ordered hard-boiled eggs to be finely chopped and mixed with mayonnaise, to fill a tomato ring. Instead, she pushed the yolks and whites separately through a sieve, saving out half a dozen halves of the whites (the eggs were cut horizontally) to use as barques for the mayonnaise. Then, on a bed of lettuce, she spread a layer of mayonnaise, one of sieved yolk, one of sieved white, etc. The result was very light, and also pretty. At the same time, the tomato ring was filled with chicken salad. It was an agreeable combination, "marrying" well. If 12 eggs are used, this salad serves six.

★

## Fruit Salad

This recipe comes from Vence, France.

Remove all peel and white pith from 8 oranges. Cut them in slices. Add 8 or 10 sliced bananas and, if in season, a couple of boxes of strawberries. Sprinkle generously with sugar. Just before serving, pour ½ bottle of champagne over all. Serves eight.

★ NOTE: *This is fruit salad as the French know it. We would serve it as dessert.* H.E.B.

★

## Leek Salad

This terse recipe was contributed to a cookbook by the Princess Bibesco, when her husband was Rumanian ambassador to Washington. I include it as being the shortest recipe I have ever seen. Good, too!

*Bibesco Salad:* Boil leeks and pour over them a mayonnaise. (!)

★

## Stuffed Lettuce

Thoroughly wash a large head of perfect young lettuce, leaving it intact. Spread each leaf with a mixture of cream cheese and Roquefort, well blended together with a little cream and seasoned with salt and pepper. Begin with the center of the lettuce and rebuild the head, stuffing carefully as you go along. Put in the refrigerator to chill. When ready to serve, slice into horizontal layers and moisten with French dressing.

★

## Lobster Salad

2 medium-sized cooked lobsters
1 pound cooked young string beans
12 small boiled potatoes
1 cup mayonnaise (or more)
2 tablespoons tomato catsup
Salt and pepper
2 hard-boiled eggs, sliced
8 tiny cooked beets

[ 179 ]

Extract meat from lobster tails and cut into thin slices. Mix with the beans, the potatoes cut in quarters or eighths, the mayonnaise and catsup, mixed together. Mix gently, adding more mayonnaise if needed. Season with salt and pepper, and arrange in a dome. Surround with egg slices and beets, alternating them. Serves six to eight.

★

## Macaroni Salad

1 pound elbow or salad macaroni
6 cooked artichoke bottoms (fonds)
2 chopped hard-boiled eggs
¼ cup minced parsley
1 cup mayonnaise (or more)
2 tablespoons tomato purée
Salt and pepper

Cook macaroni in salt water until just tender. (If long macaroni is used, tie the ends of the bunch with string and cook that way; drain and cool and cut into 1-inch lengths with a French knife.) Cut artichoke bottoms in squares and mix with the macaroni. Add other ingredients, using more mayonnaise if the mixture is too stiff. Correct seasoning and serve to six.

★

## Marquise Salad

This is very good for a luncheon *de cérémonie*.

Cut endives and slices of truffle into coarse julienne. Dress with mayonnaise en dôme and surround with celery en julienne. Sprinkle generously with chopped pistachio nuts. It is well worth the expense of the truffles (a tiny can) and the pistachio nuts, which are not cheap.

★

## Salade Mimosa

This salad is always a sure-fire success — particularly nice for a buffet.

1 ripe firm pineapple
2 cups cooked diced carrots
2 cups cooked peas
Mayonnaise
Salt and pepper
1 hard-boiled egg yolk

Cut a slice from the bottom of the pineapple and carefully scoop out the insides, leaving the wall intact. Cut flesh in dice, discarding the core; combine with carrots, peas, and enough mayonnaise to moisten well. Correct seasoning. Cut a thin slice from the side of the pineapple so it won't roll, and put on a large plate. Fill with the mixture, having the excess salad spilling out of it like a horn of plenty. Sprinkle overflow with the egg yolk forced through a sieve. Serves six to eight.

★

## Mushroom and Shrimp Salad

½ pound raw mushrooms
½ pound cooked shrimps
¼ cup sauce vinaigrette
1 teaspoon prepared mustard
1 tablespoon minced parsley
1 sliced hard-boiled egg

Wash and dry mushrooms and slice thin. Slice shrimps the same way. Mix vinaigrette with mustard, and combine with mushrooms and shrimps. Add more sauce if needed. Sprinkle with the parsley and decorate with the egg. Serves six.

★
## French Style Potato Salad

Boil spuds in their skins. To avoid having them mushy, cook
in water just under the boil, and drain while a speck under-
cooked. Plunge into cold water and peel while warm. Slice into
a salad bowl, pour over a sauce vinaigrette. Cool. Sprinkle with
minced parsley and chives.

★
## Potato Salad à la Herman Oelrichs

Cook and peel 2 pounds of potatoes as above; leave whole.
While they're still hot, pour over them ¾ cup of olive oil, turning the hot potatoes to absorb the oil. Squeeze over them the
juice of a lemon, and sprinkle with salt and freshly ground pepper. When cool, slice and sprinkle with minced parsley, chives,
tarragon, and chervil, taking care not to break the slices. Mayonnaise may be passed for those who like it.

★
## Rice Salad

This recipe is from H.R.H. Princesse Sixte do Bourbon-Parme.
Dress 4 cups of cold cooked rice lightly with French dressing. Surround with small peeled tomatoes seeded and quartered, little piles of cooked green beans, and hard-boiled egg
whites filled with mayonnaise. Garnish rice with anchovy fillets.
Serves six.

★
## Rice and Melon Salad
This is very unusual.

4 cups cooked rice
Small ripe melon, peeled, seeded and diced

[ 182 ]

Heavy cream
Lemon juice
Salt and pepper

Mix rice with melon and dress with heavy cream, lemon juice, salt and pepper to taste. "It may be decorated with nasturtium flowers," says the Comtesse de Berjane, who invented it. Serves six.

★

## Salade Russe

No two cookery books will ever give you the same ingredients for a "Russian salad," nor in any two houses will it be composed of the same things. In Russia, the term always means the inclusion of meat, such as ham or tongue, cut julienne, and anchovies. I find this sort of salad most useful, especially for a buffet or a Sunday lunch on the terrasse.

2 steamed celery roots, peeled and diced
2 cups cooked and diced carrots
2 cups cooked peas
Mayonnaise
2 cups cooked string beans
French dressing
1 pound cooked smoked tongue, cut julienne
3 hard-boiled eggs

Dress celery root, carrots and peas with mayonnaise, keeping them separate. Dress string beans with French dressing. Arrange vegetables and tongue in a bowl, keeping the ingredients in segments as carefully separated as nature does orange sections. Outline sections with the egg white cut in strips, and sprinkle the sieved yolks over the tongue. Serves eight to ten.

★
## Salade Sarah Bernhardt

This delectable salad was invented by the great Escoffier.

Wash, dry and slice a little over ½ pound of fresh firm young mushrooms. Put in a bowl with a couple of truffles cut julienne, and 2 cooked artichoke hearts, also cut julienne. Pare 4 potatoes and cut into cylinders — a form like a long large cork. Cook and slice thin. Arrange pleasantly, with asparagus tips and shrimps. Serve coated with a light mayonnaise. There you have everything, almost, but the kitchen stove, but the result is most gratifying.

★ NOTE: *To cut the potatoes easily, use a column cutter or, lacking that, an apple corer. This is more of an idea than a recipe, but certainly a good one.* H.E.B.

★
## Titania Salad

4 boiled potatoes, sliced thin
4 cooked artichoke bottoms, diced
1 cup raw sliced mushrooms
2 cups cooked baby shrimps
1 teaspoon each minced tarragon, chervil and parsley
½ cup French dressing
1 teaspoon prepared mustard
Mayonnaise
Lemon juice

Combine vegetables, shrimps and herbs. Combine French dressing and mustard, and stir in gently. Add mayonnaise and lemon juice to taste. Serves six.

★

## Tomato Mousse Ring

1 pound tomatoes, peeled and seeded
Butter
2 tablespoons flour
1 cup chicken or veal broth or consommé
2 envelopes plain gelatine
½ cup cold water
Salt, pepper and cayenne
1 cup whipping cream

Chop tomatoes and cook to a pulp with 1 tablespoon of butter. Make a roux with 2 tablespoons of butter and the flour, cook a minute, then stir in the broth. When thick and smooth, combine with tomatoes. Soak gelatine in water and dissolve over hot water. Add to mixture and season with salt, pepper and cayenne. Cool until it begins to thicken; whip the cream and fold into the mixture. Pour into a 5-cup ring mold and turn out when set. This is good filled with crab, chicken or lobster salad. Pass mayonnaise mousseline to four.

★ NOTE: *Mayonnaise mousseline is mayonnaise mixed with an equal amount of whipped cream.* H.E.B.

★

## Salad from Touraine

Remove strings from 10 nice white celery ribs. Cut them in 2½ inch lengths, and then cut them again julienne. Add 1 pound of sliced cold boiled potatoes and some of the tenderest parts from 2 heads of curly chicory. Mix with a mayonnaise slightly diluted with a little sour cream, and sprinkle with minced parsley and chervil. Be sure that the mayonnaise has a tang of mustard in it. Serves four.

★

## A Final Salad

Pick over fresh watercress. Pare the peel and pith from oranges, and then slice them. Mix watercress and oranges with a good French dressing. This is deliciously refreshing in hot weather.

★

## French Dressing

So many people have what they *call* "French dressing," and some of the concoctions are pretty extraordinary, some even weird and wonderful. A real French dressing is nothing but salt, freshly ground pepper, olive oil, and vinegar. The oil is used in a proportion of 3 tablespoons of oil to 1 of vinegar. To have a good French dressing, the oil and the vinegar must be of the *highest* quality. One great California hostess asserted that the success of the salad course could rise or fall upon the quality of the vinegar. She used aged red wine vinegar. If you want to have a delicious salad, served as it is done in France, don't, I beg of you, ever dream of adding sugar to the dressing. It is anathema! Add a little strong mustard if you will, if you like the tang which it produces, but even then you will have departed from the true principle of a real French dressing.

★ NOTE: *Some vinegars are very acid, so be sure to taste the dressing and add more oil if necessary. Four or even five parts of oil to one of vinegar may be necessary with many of today's bottled vinegars.* H.E.B.

★

## Sour Cream Sauce

At a buffet dinner that Jim Beard gave for me in New York, this was served with very thinly sliced cucumbers and very thin slices of Bermuda onion. It was a poem.

1 cup sour cream
1 tablespoon grated horseradish
2 tablespoons grated Swiss cheese
½ teaspoon salt
½ teaspoon freshly ground black pepper
1 teaspoon dry mustard

Combine ingredients and beat well.

★

## Mayonnaise

Put 6 egg yolks in a bowl with 2 teaspoons of salt and some freshly ground white pepper. Add 3 tablespoons of white wine vinegar and, beating briskly and constantly with a whip, drop in a pint (2 cups) of olive oil, starting with a few drops and gradually increasing the amount as it thickens.

★ NOTE: *This makes a large quantity — about 2½ cups. The recipe may be cut in half. Lemon juice may be used in place of vinegar, and the oil may be part (not more than half) salad oil.* H.E.B.

★

## Vinaigrette Sauce

¼ teaspoon salt
¼ teaspoon freshly ground pepper
¼ teaspoon strong mustard
3 tablespoons olive oil
1 tablespoon best wine vinegar

Mix all together with a wooden spoon.

★ NOTE: *As you see, this is what Americans call French dressing. When chopped chives, parsley, or other herbs are added, we call it "vinaigrette."* H.E.B.

★

### Estill's Wonderful Salad Dressing

Many years ago this unusual salad dressing was given to me with the remark that it was wonderful, and so, throughout the years, it has always been called just that. "Estill" is Estill Stephens Bartell.

> 4 egg yolks
> 4 tablespoons vinegar
> 1 tablespoon sugar
> 1 teaspoon salt
> 1 scant teaspoon dry mustard
> Dash of paprika
> 12 marshmallows
> 1 cup cream, whipped
> ½ cup chopped pecans (optional)

Beat the yolks light, and then add vinegar, sugar, salt, mustard, and paprika. Cook in double boiler until thick. Then remove from the fire and add the marshmallows, cut into very small bits. Cool, and just before serving, fold in the whipped cream and, if you like the idea, ½ cup of chopped pecans. This is served over peeled tinned apricot halves, drained of their syrup, and makes a most unusual dessert. You may wish to add more sugar to the recipe; the vinegar and salt make for a baffling flavor. Excellent on all fruit salads.

DESSERTS,
CAKES
and COOKIES

DESSERTS
CAKES
and COOKIES

★
## Perfect Pie Crust

 2 cups sifted flour
 1 teaspoon salt
 ⅔ cup lard
 2 tablespoons butter
 Ice water

 Work the first four ingredients well with fingertips until the mixture resembles meal. Work quickly. Add enough ice water to bind, about ¼ cup. Roll into a ball, cover with waxed paper, and let stand in the refrigerator overnight. Enough for a 9-inch, 2-crust pie.

★
## Cream Cookies

 1 cup butter
 2 cups sugar
 2 eggs
 1 cup sour cream
 1 teaspoon vanilla
 1 teaspoon salt
 Flour (6 to 7 cups)
 1 egg white
 1 tablespoon milk
 Ground nuts or cinnamon and sugar (optional)

 Cream butter and sugar, add eggs and mix well, then add sour cream, vanilla, salt, and enough flour to make a dough that one can roll. Roll to proper thinness, cut in rounds, and brush tops with egg white slightly beaten with milk. Sprinkle with ground nuts, or cinnamon and sugar, if you wish. Bake at 350° for 7 to 8 minutes, or until nicely browned.

★ NOTE: *Mr. Veach says this recipe will make about 60 cookies; I got almost 500 2¼-inch ones. Obviously, we don't agree about "proper thinness." If you don't like them paper-thin, as I do, allow a longer baking time. H.E.B.*

★
## Nut Cookies

¼ cup (½ bar) butter
1 cup brown sugar
2 tablespoons flour
1 egg, separated
1 cup finely chopped walnuts

Cream butter and sugar; add flour, beaten egg yolk, and nuts. Mix well. Beat egg white until stiff, and fold in. Drop by scant half-teaspoons on well-buttered cookie sheets, leaving space for spreading. Bake in a 350° oven for 7 to 9 minutes, taking great care, as they burn easily. Let stand a few seconds, then remove from pans immediately. If they stick, slip back into the oven to warm for a few seconds. These are tricky, but worth the trouble. Makes 30 cookies.

★
## Chatillon

3 cups flour
½ pound butter
3 egg yolks

[ 192 ]

¼ cup sugar
1 tablespoon cream

Mix all ingredients together until well blended, and divide equally among four 8-inch layer cake pans which have been lined with buttered paper. Press dough evenly into uniform thickness, and bake in a 350° oven for 15 minutes, or until pale gold. Cool before removing from pans. Spread a layer with crème pâtissière, top with another layer, which spread with currant jelly, and repeat, having the next layer crème and the top one jelly. Cover all with crème à la vanille. This disappears like magic.

★ NOTE: *If you don't have the four pans, press the dough on foil which has been marked with 8-inch circles, and bake on cookie sheets. These layers break easily, so take care, but a crack or two is no great disaster as the crème will cover all flaws. If you don't want to bother with making the two crèmes, simply thin some of the crème pâtissière with cream in place of the crème à la vanille. In that case, increase the recipe by one-half. H.E.B.*

★

## Crème à la Vanille

2 cups rich milk
¼ cup sugar
4 egg yolks
1 teaspoon vanilla

Heat milk with sugar, stirring until dissolved. Beat egg yolks until light, and gradually add hot milk. Cook in a double boiler over hot, not boiling, water until thickened and the cream coats a silver spoon. Add vanilla and cool. Don't let this mixture get too hot or it will curdle.

[ 193 ]

★

## *Crème Pâtissière*

A custard sauce, somewhat thicker than English custard.

½ cup flour
½ cup sugar
¼ cup melted butter
Pinch of salt
4 eggs
2 cups scalded milk or thin cream
1 teaspoon vanilla

Mix together flour, sugar, butter, salt and eggs, then gradually beat in hot milk or cream. Cook over hot water, stirring occasionally, until thick and smooth. Cool slightly and add vanilla. Makes almost 4 cups.

★

## *Crème Anglaise*

3 eggs or 6 egg yolks
¼ cup sugar
⅛ teaspoon salt
2 cups scalded milk or thin cream
½ teaspoon vanilla

Beat eggs to blend well, add sugar and salt, and pour in scalded milk. Cook in a double boiler, stirring constantly, until the mixture coats a spoon. Keep the water in the bottom of the boiler just under the boil — overheating will cause the mixture to curdle. Cool and add vanilla.

★

## *Crépy*

This recipe, from the Baronne de Crépy, is a French gâteau au chocolat, very different from American chocolate cakes.

Rich and moist, it needs no icing, but is delicious cut in small pieces and served with whipped cream for dessert.

> ½ cup (¼ pound) butter
> ½ cup chocolate (see Note)
> 3 eggs, separated
> ½ cup sugar
> 3 tablespoons flour
> ¼ cup grated almonds

Line a pan 8 inches in diameter and at least 1¼ inches high with buttered paper. Melt butter and chocolate together over hot water. Remove from heat, beat in egg yolks, sugar, flour and almonds. (Whirl almonds in a blender or grate them in a rotary grater.) Then beat egg whites stiff and fold in. Pour into prepared pan and bake at 425° for 16 minutes. Cool, invert on a cake rack, and peel off paper. Serves six to eight.

★ NOTE: *French chocolate is quite different from ours. Mr. Veach says he sometimes uses Menier's chocolate broken into tiny bits, sometimes powdered chocolate. I found a mixture of semisweet and unsweetened chocolate best — 2 ounces of the first and 3 ounces of the second, or vice versa, depending upon how sweet your tooth is.* H.E.B.

★

## Ice Box Dessert

> 2 dozen lady fingers
> ½ cup sweet butter
> 1 cup powdered sugar
> 4 eggs, separated
> ½ cup pulverized stale macaroons
> 1 tablespoon Jamaica rum
> 1 cup whipping cream

Line a 1½- or 2-quart mold with lady fingers. Cream butter with sugar, beat in egg yolks one at a time, add macaroons and rum, then fold in the egg whites, which have been beaten until stiff. Fill mold, cover, and chill at least 12 hours. Turn out and cover with the cream, which has been whipped and sweetened very slightly or not at all. Serves six to eight.

★

## Linzer Torte

1 cup (½ pound) butter
1 cup sugar
2 egg yolks
½ pound (1½ cups) unblanched almonds
Grated rind of 1 lemon
2 cups flour
1 tablespoon cinnamon
½ teaspoon cloves
Raspberry jam

Cream butter and sugar until light; beat in egg yolks. Grind almonds, using finest blade, and add to mixture along with lemon rind, flour and spices, and mix well. Reserve one-third of the mixture, and press remaining into an 8- by 8-inch pan (or use an 8- or 9-inch flan ring or spring mold). Line the bottom and about ½ inch up the sides of the pan, having the bottom the thickest. Spread with raspberry jam, preferably the seedless variety. Roll remaining dough on a floured board and cut into narrow strips. Lay over the torte in lattice fashion. Bake in a 350° oven for 40 minutes, or until nicely browned. Cool and cut in squares.

★ NOTE: *This famous Austrian dessert is well worth the trouble. The strips may be brushed with slightly beaten egg white before baking.* H.E.B.

★
## Old-Fashioned Cream Cake

½ cup (¼ pound) butter
1¼ cups sugar
Grated rind of 1 lemon
¼ cup Cognac
4 eggs, separated
1½ cups cake flour
½ teaspoon salt
1 teaspoon baking powder
⅛ teaspoon baking soda

Cream butter and sugar until light; add lemon rind, Cognac, and well-beaten egg yolks. Sift dry ingredients together and add, alternating with the egg whites, which have been beaten stiff. Divide between two 8- or 9-inch layer cake pans, and bake in a 350° oven for about 30 minutes, or until a pick comes out clean. Cool the layers and put together with cream rum filling. Sift powdered sugar over top.

★
## Cream Rum Filling

1 cup thin cream
¼ cup flour
⅓ cup sugar
⅛ teaspoon salt
1 egg
2 tablespoons Jamaica rum

Scald ¾ cup of the cream. Mix remaining with the flour and add, along with sugar and salt. Cook, stirring, until thickened. Beat egg and stir in some of the hot mixture, then add to remaining mixture. Cook over low heat, stirring constantly, until thick and smooth. Cool slightly and add rum.

[ 197 ]

★

## Childhood Memory

Bake 2 squares of simple sponge cake, fill with crème pâtissière, and sprinkle top with powdered sugar.

★ NOTE: *Bill Veach doesn't say so, but I suspect that this was a very pleasant childhood memory!* H.E.B.

★

## Potato Cake

For me this is the best of them all. Once, serving it at tea in France, when all were loud in their praise of the cake (and helped themselves accordingly), I was asked what went into the making. I recounted. One lady present, paying scant attention, overheard the words "mashed potatoes." "*Quel horreur!*" she exclaimed, throwing her hands up in purely Gallic distaste. "But you have just said you wanted the recipe for the cake, Madame," I replied. It was conceded that the potatoes replace some of the flour, and the agitated marquise took a back seat — and the recipe!

> 1 cup (½ pound) butter
> 2 cups sugar
> 2 cups flour (sometimes a little more)
> 4 large eggs
> 1 cup milk
> 1 cup chopped walnuts
> ½ cup (4 ounces) grated unsweetened chocolate
> 1 cup hot mashed potatoes
> 1 tablespoon baking powder
> 1 teaspoon *each:* cinnamon, allspice, ginger, mace
> ½ teaspoon cloves
> 1 teaspoon vanilla

Cream butter and sugar. Add the other ingredients, beating well. Pour into a large cake tin (see Note) containing a buttered paper lining. Bake in a moderately hot oven (375°) until a broom straw, stuck down the center, comes out clean — about 45 minutes. The Queen of Cakes!

★ NOTE: *This makes one cake 10 by 14 inches, or one 9 by 9 plus a loaf pan, or three loaf pans. This cake is an old-time favorite on the West Coast. It is marvelously moist and keeps well.* H.E.B.

★
## Pound Cake

Well do I remember my eighth birthday, and the splendid party which my charming mother gave to celebrate it. It fell on Valentine's Day, and the house was decorated with garlands and festoons of red hearts. Even the ice cream was heart-shaped. The birthday cake, which was the most enormous cake I think I ever saw outside of wedding cakes, was also marvelously good.

> 1 pound butter
> 2 cups sugar
> 10 eggs
> 1 teaspoon nutmeg
> 1 teaspoon pineapple flavoring (or vanilla or almond)
> 4 cups flour
> 2 teaspoons baking powder

Cream butter and sugar together. Separate the eggs and beat yolks and whites. Add the yolks to the creamed butter and sugar, then fold in the stiffly beaten whites, adding also the nutmeg and flavoring. Now stir in rapidly the flour, sifted with the baking powder. Pour into a large cake pan (see Note) lined with buttered paper, and bake in a slow oven (300°) for about an hour, or until a pick comes out clean. Cool and then frost, if desired.

★ NOTE: *Use a 10- by 14-inch pan, or a 12-inch round pan. I am not sure why Bill Veach adds baking powder to this pound cake, but it does no harm. Two loaf pans may be used, in which case bake 10 minutes longer.* H.E.B.

★

## Tea Cake

1 egg
¼ cup sugar
¾ cup milk
½ cup melted butter
2 cups flour, sifted with
1 tablespoon baking powder
Sugar, cinnamon and butter for topping

Mix thoroughly all except topping ingredients and turn into 2 buttered 9-inch pie tins. Cover the tops of each with a generous handful of sugar and plenty of cinnamon shaken from the tin. Dot top well with peas of butter, about a dozen to each top. Bake 12 to 15 minutes in a moderate oven (350°). Let cool a little before trying to cut, but it is excellent eaten warm. It is very good, too, with morning coffee.

★

## Visitandines

This is truly French, a delightful petit four sec to serve with tea, or with fruit or ice cream desserts.

1 cup sugar
½ cup (¼ pound) butter

1 cup flour
½ cup grated blanched almonds
4 egg whites

Cream sugar and butter; add flour and almonds; mix, and add egg whites, beaten stiff. Combine thoroughly. Fill well-buttered barquette pans ⅔ full, and bake in a 350° oven for 10 or 15 minutes or until golden.

★ NOTE: *This makes about 50 little elliptical cakes, 3 inches long and 1 inch wide at the bottom. Tiny tart pans may be used.* H.E.B.

★

## Old-Fashioned Deep Apple Pie

6 to 8 large tart apples
¾ cup sugar
½ teaspoon cinnamon
¼ teaspoon nutmeg
2 teaspoons flour
4 tablespoons (½ bar) butter

Butter a casserole or deep baking dish, one holding about 2½ quarts. Slice the peeled apples into it, sprinkling each layer with some of the sugar, cinnamon and nutmeg, flour and butter. Cover with rich pie crust, making several incisions in the top for the steam to escape. Bake in a 450° oven for 10 minutes, reduce heat to 350°, and bake for 40 minutes, or until the crust is brown and the apples are tender. Serves six.

★

## Rich Pie Crust

1¼ cups flour
½ teaspoon salt
1 teaspoon baking powder

¾ cup shortening
3 to 4 tablespoons ice water

Sift flour with salt and baking powder. Work in shortening (lard is best) with fingertips, and slowly add water. Form into a ball, wrap in waxed paper, and chill several hours before rolling.

★ NOTE: *If you don't like the idea of using all lard, try half butter.* H.E.B.

★

### Pommes Portugaise

8 slices good white bread
½ pound butter
8 large firm apples
16 cubes (or ⅓ cup) sugar
Apricot marmalade
Cream

Cut bread in 2½- to 3-inch rounds, spread very generously on one side with butter, and arrange on a baking dish that can come to the table. Peel and core the apples and place one on each round of bread. Put 2 cubes (or 2 teaspoons) of sugar in the cavity of each and fill to the top with butter. Bake in a 350° oven for 30 to 40 minutes, or until the apples are brown and tender, basting with more butter if necessary. Before serving, fill each cavity with apricot marmalade. Pass thin cream. Serves eight.

★

### Bananas Beauharnais

3 tablespoons butter
8 firm bananas
¼ cup sugar

[ 202 ]

2 tablespoons white rum
1½ cups heavy cream
1 cup stale macaroon crumbs

Spread a flat baking dish with the butter. Peel bananas and arrange in the dish; sprinkle with the sugar and rum. Put in a 450° oven for 5 minutes, pour the cream over them, sprinkle with the macaroon crumbs, and return to the oven long enough to become golden. Serves eight.

★

## Bavarian Cream

1 cup milk or cream
2 eggs, separated
2 tablespoons sugar
Pinch of salt
1 envelope gelatine
¼ cup cold water
1 cup whipping cream
3 tablespoons powdered sugar
¾ teaspoon vanilla

Scald milk or cream. Beat egg yolks with sugar and salt, and gradually add milk. Cook, stirring, until thickened. Soak gelatine in cold water and add to custard. Cool until it begins to thicken, then add egg whites that have been beaten stiff. Whip cream, add sugar and vanilla, and fold into mixture. Pour into a 1½-quart mold and refrigerate. Serves six.

★

## Bavarian Charlotte (Charlotte Russe)

Make as above, but use a 2-quart mold lined with lady fingers.

★
## Carrot Pudding

I believe this recipe is similar to a carrot pudding made at the Pacific Union Club in San Francisco.

> 1 cup grated raw carrots
> 1 cup grated raw potatoes
> 1 teaspoon baking soda
> 1 cup sugar
> 1 cup dried currants
> 1 cup raisins
> 1 cup flour
> ¼ cup (½ bar) butter
> ½ teaspoon cinnamon
> ½ teaspoon cloves
> ½ teaspoon nutmeg

Mix together and pour into a greased 1½-quart mold. Cover and steam for 3½ hours. Unmold and serve to eight.

★ NOTE: *This may be served flaming with Cognac or rum, or with a thin vanilla or rum sauce, or whipped cream.* H.E.B.

★
## Caramelized Walnuts

The best time of the year to make these delicious, delectable dainties is when the walnuts are just off the trees; then they can be easily brushed of their skins.

Remove the shells carefully, which is best done by inserting the point of a penknife into the stem end of the nut. If the nuts are soft-shelled, the shells will part company very easily, and you will have no difficulty in obtaining two perfect halves. Brush with a little stiff brush to remove the skins.

Pour boiling water on the nuts and soak for 1 minute; drain and roll in granulated sugar, so that the nuts are evenly but not thickly coated with the sugar. Let dry overnight, then put a single layer in a frying basket and cook in deep fat, preferably peanut or olive oil, heated to 380°; the sugar will caramelize at once. Quickly remove the nuts and put in some more. These are wonderfully good. A small candy box filled with these little treasures makes a most delightful and personal gift.

★ NOTE: *As most of us can't get walnuts "just off the trees," I buy shelled walnut halves and put them in a 450° oven for 5 minutes. If the brown skins do not brush off easily, return them to the oven for another few minutes. H.E.B.*

★

## *Charlotte of Apples and Apricots*

6 large firm apples
2 tablespoons butter
¼ cup sugar
½ teaspoon vanilla
1 cup stewed apricots
4 to 6 brioches
Butter

Peel and slice apples and cook in butter until golden brown. Add sugar and vanilla and stir into a sauce. Add the apricots, which have been sweetened to taste, and mix well. Slice brioches about ¼ inch thick and butter generously on both sides. Line a 1½-quart mold with them, pour in fruit mixture, top with additional brioche slices, and bake in a 350° oven for 45 minutes, or until the brioche slices are crisp and brown. Turn out and serve warm or cold with whipped cream or crème Anglaise. Serves six.

★
## Chocolate Soufflé

4 squares unsweetened chocolate
¼ cup milk
3 egg yolks
½ cup sugar
6 egg whites
¼ teaspoon salt

Put chocolate and milk in the top of a double boiler, and cook over boiling water until the chocolate is melted. Beat egg yolks with 3 tablespoons of the sugar until light. Combine with chocolate. Beat egg whites until stiff, add remaining sugar and salt, and fold into chocolate mixture. Turn into a 1- or 1½-quart buttered soufflé dish and bake in a 350° oven for 20 minutes. Serve at once to four.

★ NOTE: *This has a delightfully runny center that serves as a sauce, in the French manner. If you prefer it set all the way through, cook 5 to 10 minutes longer.* H.E.B.

★
## Cold Lemon Soufflé

6 eggs, separated
⅔ cup sugar
1 tablespoon plain gelatine
Juice of 2 lemons
2 tablespoons currant jelly

Beat egg yolks with sugar, add gelatine softened in the lemon juice, and cook over hot water, stirring, until it thickens. Cool. Beat egg whites stiff and fold into mixture; pile into a glass dish and chill. Decorate with dabs of currant jelly and serve with lady fingers. Serves six.

---

★
## Crème Brûlée

1 quart heavy cream
8 egg yolks
Brown sugar
½ teaspoon salt

Scald cream. Beat yolks with ½ cup brown sugar and salt, and beat in the cream gradually. Cook over hot water, whipping constantly, until the mixture thickens and will coat a silver spoon. Take great care not to overcook, as the mixture will curdle. Pour into a 1½- or 2-quart baking dish and chill for several hours or overnight. About 4 hours before serving, cover with an even layer of brown sugar ¼ inch thick. Put under a broiler so that the sugar will melt and caramelize. Watch carefully, and turn so that the top will be evenly glazed. Return to the refrigerator until serving time. Serves six or eight.

This was one of King Edward VII's favorite desserts, and is also a favorite of Queen Helen, Queen Mother of Rumania.

★
## Crème au Chocolat en Petits Pots

This recipe, which is that of the Marquise de Pins, is so good and so simple and easy to prepare that all houses should be equipped with the charming little porcelain or earthenware pots, with covers, especially made for this purpose.

5 ounces semisweet chocolate
2 tablespoons butter
5 tablespoons sugar
5 eggs, separated
1 teaspoon vanilla

# A BON VIVANT'S COOKBOOK

Melt chocolate in double boiler over hot, not boiling, water. Add butter and sugar, working with a wooden spatula. When creamy, remove from heat and beat in the egg yolks. Add vanilla and fold in the egg whites, beaten stiff but not dry. Divide among 6 petits pots. Serves six.

★ NOTE: *Unsweetened chocolate may be used, in which case increase the sugar to ⅔ cup. The butter may also be increased to 6 tablespoons (¾ bar) if calories concern you not at all.* H.E.B.

★

## Molded Eggnog

1 envelope plain gelatine
½ cup sugar
⅛ teaspoon salt
2 cups milk or thin cream
3 eggs, separated
¼ cup sherry
⅛ teaspoon nutmeg
Shredded coconut

Combine gelatine, sugar, salt, and milk in the top of a double boiler. Place over medium heat and stir until the gelatine dissolves. Remove from heat. Beat egg yolks slightly, and gradually add hot milk. Return the mixture to the top of the double boiler and cook over hot, not boiling, water, stirring constantly, for 10 minutes, or until the custard coats a silver spoon. Remove from heat and add sherry and nutmeg. Chill until it begins to thicken, then add egg whites, beaten stiff but not dry. Pour into a 1½-quart mold and chill. Unmold and cover top

[ 208 ]

with shredded coconut, preferably fresh. Serves six to eight.

★

## Fresh Fig Mousse

Delicious! But rich as all get-out. Go ahead and enjoy it —
but not every day.

> 18 large ripe figs
> 1 cup sugar
> 2 cups whipping cream
> 1 cup powdered sugar
> ¼ teaspoon almond extract

Peel figs and slice enough to make 5 cups. (Keep remainder
well covered for a garnish.) Sprinkle with sugar and let stand
until it dissolves. Drain off juice. Whip cream and add powdered sugar and almond extract. Put a layer of cream in a 2½-
quart mold. Follow with a layer of figs, repeating until all is
used (the top layer should be cream). Freeze in ice and rock
salt for 4 hours (or in the freezer overnight). Unmold and
decorate with the peeled figs, in which you've stuck a little
strip of angélique or a blanched almond to simulate a stem.

★

## Ripe Figs with Raspberries

Peel the desired number of ripe figs. Make a hole in the top
of each and fill with a teaspoon of raspberry jam. Pour a dessert
spoon of port over each fig, and cover all with whipped cream.
Augment with fresh raspberries, if you want something really
wonderful, in which case less of the port.

★ NOTE: *I surrounded the figs with fresh raspberries — a truly
delectable dessert.* H.E.B.

[ 209 ]

★

## Figs with Strawberries

Surround a large mound of handsome luscious strawberries
with a border of ripe peeled white figs. Sprinkle a little sugar
over all, and put a blanched almond in the end of each fig to
look like a stem. Pass cream.

★

## Grapefruit with Strawberry Sauce

The combination of the tangy fresh fruit and the sweetness
of the sauce is very refreshing. What's more, the yellow-green
of the grapefruit showing through the pink of the sauce is very
pleasing to the eye.

Carefully remove segments from the desired number of
grapefruit (allow 1 for each 2 servings) so that none of the
pith is present (see Oranges in Glossary). Just before serving,
cover with chilled strawberry sauce.

★

## Strawberry Sauce

Crush ripe strawberries and pass through a sieve. Put in a
saucepan, adding 1 cup of sugar for each cup of purée. Cook
until the sugar is thoroughly dissolved. Chill before pouring
over grapefruit.

★

## Lemon Cream

6 eggs, separated
2 large lemons
1 cup sugar

Beat egg yolks slightly. Add the grated rind of 1 lemon,
the juice of both, and the sugar. Cook over hot water, stirring,

until thick. Cool slightly, add stiffly beaten egg whites, combining thoroughly. Pour into a pretty serving dish and chill thoroughly. Serve as is, with a simple cake without icing, or plain cookies. Serves six.

★

## Old-Fashioned Lemon Pie

1 baked 8-inch pie shell
3 eggs, separated
Sugar
2 lemons
1 cup finely sieved cracker crumbs (about 24 saltines)
1 cup boiling water
2 tablespoons butter

Beat egg yolks slightly, beat in ¾ cup of sugar, the grated rind of 1 lemon and the juice of both, the cracker crumbs, water and butter. Cook over hot water, stirring, until thick. Cool slightly, then pour into the baked pie shell. When cool, cover with a meringue made with the egg whites and 6 tablespoons of sugar. Put in a 400° oven until nicely colored, about 5 minutes. Serves four to six.

★

## Maple Bisque

5 egg yolks
1 cup pure maple syrup
1 envelope plain gelatine
1½ cups whipping cream

Beat egg yolks lightly and add maple syrup. Soften gelatine in 3 tablespoons of the cream and add, then cook over hot

# A BON VIVANT'S COOKBOOK

water until thickened, stirring occasionally. Cool thoroughly, then whip cream and fold in. Pour into a 1½-quart mold and chill. Serves four.

★ NOTE: *This is delicious but rich. I don't believe it would be parsimonious to serve it to six. Some simple cake or cookie, or perhaps lady fingers, would go well here. H.E.B.*

★

## Mousse au Café

Blanch and sliver 1 cup of almonds, then gild in 2 tablespoons of butter, sprinkling with a teaspoon of sugar to give extra color. Unmold 1½ quarts of rich coffee mousse on a plate, sprinkle with the almonds, and pass hot chocolate sauce, or serve with crème de cacao. Either is sensational. Serves six to eight.

★

## Hot Chocolate Sauce

Melt 5 ounces of good milk chocolate in a double boiler with 3 tablespoons of very strong after-dinner coffee. Stir until smooth.

★

## Rich Coffee Mousse

¾ cup sugar
½ cup very strong coffee
5 egg yolks
2 cups whipping cream
Few grains salt

Combine sugar and coffee and simmer for 8 minutes. Beat egg yolks until thick, gradually beat the coffee mixture into them, and cook over hot water, stirring, until thick. Cool. Whip cream, add salt, and fold into other mixture. Pour into a 1½-quart mold, cover, seal well, and pack in 2 parts of chopped ice to 1 part of rock salt for 4 hours, or freeze in coldest part of freezer overnight.

★

### Bread Soufflé

1 loaf (1 pound) bread
1 quart milk
½ cup sugar
3 eggs, separated
½ cup (¼ pound) butter
2 teaspoons vanilla

Cut crust from bread, break in chunks, cover with milk, and let stand overnight. Press out excess milk, add the sugar, egg yolks, and the butter, which should be very soft but not melted. Mix well. Beat the egg whites until stiff and add, along with the vanilla. Pour into a buttered 2½-quart soufflé dish and bake in a 350° oven for an hour, or until set and brown. Serve with any dessert sauce, or with stewed fruit or preserves. Serves eight.

★

### Oranges and Coconut

This homely dessert was a favorite of my grandmother's.

Peel oranges with a very sharp knife, deeply enough to remove both rinds and all vestiges of white pith. Slice the globes horizontally into a bowl, sprinkling with a very little sugar, and covering each layer of fruit with a slight covering of shredded coconut. Add a little Curaçao, if you wish.

[ 213 ]

★
## Oranges à la Ritz

This is a most welcome dessert after a rich meal. Peel one large orange for each guest, taking care to remove all pith. Cut half of them in halves, horizontally, and arrange dome side up in a serving dish. Coat with orange marmalade, and surround with the remaining oranges cut in segments (see Glossary). Serve chilled.

★ NOTE: *Far be it from me to try to improve upon a recipe from the Ritz, but I've tried this with Curaçao, Cointreau, and Triple Sec, and find them all superb.* H.E.B.

★
## Orange Rice

1 cup rice
2½ cups hot milk
1 envelope gelatine
½ cup cream
2 egg yolks
¼ cup (½ bar) butter
1 teaspoon salt
⅓ cup sugar
1 lemon
2 oranges

Cover rice with boiling water and simmer 5 minutes. Drain; put in top of a double boiler with the hot milk and cook over hot water for 45 minutes, or until the rice is tender. Soften gelatine in cream, add egg yolks, butter, salt, sugar, juice of the lemon, grated rind of 1 orange, and juice of both. Cook over low heat, stirring, until thick. Combine with rice and pour into a dish holding 1½ quarts. Chill and serve with heavy cream. Serves six.

★ NOTE: *This is a filling dessert, rather like old-fashioned rice pudding.* H.E.B.

★
## Peaches à la Condé

1 cup rice
2½ cups hot milk
1 No. 2½ can peach halves
6 tablespoons apricot jam
Angélique
Candied cherries

Cook the rice as for orange rice, first in boiling water, then with the hot milk. Don't overcook. Drain peaches. Reduce syrup to 1½ cups; add the apricot jam and stir well; cool. Arrange cooled rice in a mound on a serving dish, arrange peach halves around it, and pour syrup over all. Little green "stems" of angélique may be stuck in the top of the peaches to make the dish more stylish, and a few *candied* cherries may be dotted about for further color. But in any of my dishes, never *never*, NEVER a Maraschino cherry. *Je vous en prie!* Please! *Per favore è piacere! Entschuldigern Sie mich! Bitte!*

★
## Peaches Cardinale

8 whole white peaches
4 cups sugar
2 cups water
1 teaspoon vanilla
½ cup currant jelly
2 to 3 tablespoons kirsch
1 quart strawberry ice
Large whole strawberries (at least 8)

The peaches should be ripe yet firm. Dip in boiling water for a minute and rub off skins. Combine sugar and water and bring to a boil. Simmer 2 minutes, then add vanilla and peaches, and poach until tender. Take care that they don't fall apart! Chill. Melt jelly and beat in kirsch. Arrange strawberry ice on a platter or shallow dish, drain peaches and lay around ice. Pour the jelly over the peaches, and further decorate with the strawberries. Lay a full-blown red rose at one side of the dish before serving. Serves eight.

★

## Peaches Isabelle

Arrange peaches on strawberry ice, as above, and cover with a purée of fresh raspberries.

★ NOTE: *Whirl raspberries in a blender, strain, and sweeten to taste. Frozen raspberries may be used.* H.E.B.

★

## Peach Mousse

4 to 6 large freestone peaches (enough for 2 cups ripe
    peach pulp)
¾ cup sugar
Few grains salt
¼ teaspoon almond extract
1 envelope gelatine
⅓ cup cold water
1 quart heavy cream

Peel peaches and put through a sieve or food mill. Work quickly, adding sugar as soon as they are puréed, as they discolor quickly. Add salt, almond extract, and gelatine, which has been soaked in the water and melted over hot water. Whip cream, fold into peach mixture, and pour into a 2- or 2½-quart mold. Freeze in ice and salt (see rich coffee mousse) or in the freezer. This is very good indeed. Serves six to eight.

★

## Pancake Dessert

This most remarkable recipe, dating from the days of Charles V, is a gentle reminder that there were amazingly delicate dishes served in those faraway days, which we sometimes think of as before the advent of haute cuisine.

> 6 eggs, separated
> ⅓ cup sugar
> ½ cup (1 bar) melted butter
> ⅔ cup hot milk
> Butter
> Apricot jam

Beat egg yolks with sugar; add melted butter and hot milk. Let eggs begin to thicken (see Note), and then cool. Beat egg whites stiff and fold into the mixture. Cook, a tablespoonful at a time, in a little butter, turning carefully when lightly brown on one side. When the second side colors, slide onto a plate and spread with thin (melted) apricot jam. Build up your cake in layers, cut in wedges like a pie, and serve with whipped cream.

★ NOTE: *I found these exceedingly tricky. The author said the egg mixture would thicken, but I found it did so only if I cooked it over low heat, stirring constantly. The well-beaten egg whites make the mixture soufflé-like, and turning the pancake can be done, but not easily. However, they are light as a cloud and worth the effort. I did find that adding ¼ cup of flour to the egg yolk mixture made the whole process less frustrating, though I fear Bill Veach doesn't ap-*

[ 217 ]

*prove. I also found three or four smaller stacks easier to handle than one big one. Good luck!* H.E.B.

★

### Pears Belle Hélène

The French Line's *Liberté* made this dish famous.

Pack vanilla ice cream into a melon mold, then unmold on a platter. Arrange tinned pear halves around it and decorate with swirls of whipped cream forced through a pastry bag. Pass hot chocolate sauce.

★ NOTE: *1½ quarts of ice cream, a No. 2½ tin of pears, 1 cup of cream, whipped, and 1½ cups of chocolate sauce will serve six.* H.E.B.

★

### Pears on Croûtons

Peel pears, not too ripe, cut in half lengthwise, and remove cores. Sauté carefully in butter, sprinkling them with sugar. Fry oval pieces of bread in butter, and when pears are cooked, lay a pear half on each croûton. Pour juices from the pan over them and serve at once. Take care that the fruit does not burn or become mushy. Rather firm pears will obviate this.

★

### Pineapple with Kirsch

1 No. 2½ can pineapple
½ cup kirsch
3 egg yolks
3 tablespoons sugar
¼ pound butter
½ cup toasted shredded almonds

Drain canned pineapple (slices, cubes, or sticks — I rather prefer the latter) and marinate in kirsch, turning several times to let the fruit imbibe the liquor well. Put egg yolks in the top of a double boiler; add the sugar, butter, and kirsch drained from the pineapple. Cook over hot water, stirring, until thickened, adding pineapple juice to make a pouring consistency. Take care not to overcook, as it will curdle. Cool, pour over pineapple, and sprinkle with almonds. Serves six.

★ NOTE: *This sauce is a rich one that is also delicious on strawberries or other fresh fruit.* H.E.B.

★

## Marquise de Pruneaux

This is from the family cookbook of the Comtesse de Felcourt, of Paris.

> 1 pound best prunes
> ¾ cup (1½ bars) butter
> 2 egg yolks
> 1 tablespoon sugar
> Few grains salt
> 1 cup whipping cream

Remove pits from prunes and cook in as little water as possible until tender. Force through a food mill. This should be very thick — if not, cook further until it is. Cool. Cream the butter; add egg yolks, sugar and salt. Line a quart bowl with buttered paper. Thoroughly mix puréed prunes and egg yolk mixture. Put in prepared bowl, cover with a plate, and weigh plate with something heavy. Chill in the refrigerator for 24 hours. Unmold, remove paper, and cover with the cream, which has been whipped but not sweetened.

★ NOTE: *I found the paper lining unnecessary. The dessert*

*can easily be unmolded by dipping quickly in hot water
before inverting.* H.E.B.

★

## Pumpkin Pie

1 unbaked 9-inch pie shell
1 cup sugar
1 tablespoon flour
½ teaspoon salt
1 teaspoon ground ginger
¾ teaspoon cinnamon
⅛ teaspoon nutmeg
2 cups strained cooked pumpkin (canned may be used)
1½ tablespoons molasses
1½ tablespoons melted butter
3 eggs
1¾ cups milk
2 tablespoons brandy or whiskey

Mix sugar, flour, salt, ginger, cinnamon, and nutmeg in a
large bowl. Add pumpkin, molasses and butter. Slightly beat
eggs and add them to the milk along with the brandy or whiskey, then pour into the pumpkin mixture and blend well. Pour
the above into the waiting pie crust, unbaked, and put in a
425° oven for 35 to 40 minutes, or until a knife, inserted near
the center, comes out clean. Serve with whipped cream.

★

## Royal Soufflé

This is a spectacular dessert — a crown savarin filled with
a soufflé mixture. If you have access to a really good pastry
shop, ask them to bake the savarin for you, though it isn't diffi-

cult to make yourself. Serve this dessert when you want to show off.

### CROWN SAVARIN

1 cup flour
½ cake yeast
6 tablespoons warm milk
2 eggs
3 tablespoons butter
1 teaspoon sugar
¼ teaspoon salt

Warm a mixing bowl, put the flour in it, and make a well in the center. Add the yeast to the milk and stir until the yeast is dissolved; pour into the well. Add eggs and stir, mixing in the flour as you go along. Beat vigorously for 3 minutes, cover, and put in a warm place to rise until double in bulk. Beat the butter to a soft cream, add sugar and salt, then add to the risen dough. Pick the dough up with the fingertips and throw it back into the bowl, repeating for 5 minutes. Put into a very well buttered 4- or 5-cup ring mold and let rise to the top of the pan. Then bake in a hot (375° to 400°) oven for 20 minutes, or until a pick comes out clean. Cool slightly, then unmold on a fireproof round plate. Spoon the syrup (see below) over it carefully so that it will be absorbed. Fill center with soufflé mixture (see below), mounding it into a cone shape with a spatula. Put into a 375° oven until the soufflé is gilded. Serve at once to four.

### SYRUP

1 cup sugar
1½ cups water
2 tablespoons apricot preserves, puréed
2 tablespoons kirsch

[ 221 ]

Cook sugar and water until it begins to thicken. Add apricot; cool and add kirsch.

SOUFFLÉ

> 3 egg whites
> 3 tablespoons apricot preserves, puréed

Beat egg whites until stiff; fold in the apricot purée, and bake in the Savarin as described above.

★ NOTE: *You'll like this. All can be done ahead except for the soufflé, but the egg whites can be waiting in a bowl, and the apricot preserves already forced through a food mill, ready for the last-minute ritual. H.E.B.*

★

## Shortcakes

Living in Europe as long as I have, I have found a gratifying interest in our shortcakes, unquestionably an American institution. I think that even the informal appearance of the "cake" pleases Europeans, where chefs perfectionize everything as much as possible. In any case, when I serve a shortcake, in either France or Italy, I have an instant response of appreciation. The following recipe for shortcake is a lulu, to my way of thinking, but it is very delicate, and difficult to roll out and get into the pan.

> 2 cups flour
> 3 teaspoons baking powder
> ½ teaspoon salt
> 1 tablespoon sugar
> A little nutmeg
> Soft butter
> Milk

Sift flour with baking powder, salt, sugar and nutmeg. Work in ½ cup butter with floured fingertips. Stir in *enough milk only* to hold together, doing this little by little, so you don't overdo the milk. If the butter is quite soft, I find that I need use only ⅓ cup of milk, or very little more. Turn out on a floured board. Cut the ball of dough in half. Roll one half and place in a buttered 9-inch pie tin. Spread the top generously with softened butter. Roll out the other half and place on top of the first half. Bake 12 minutes in a 425° oven. In separating the two halves, use the utmost caution, for the cake is easily breakable. Best to let it cool a few minutes before this operation.

For filling, we all know who is queen — the strawberry. Slice and sugar them for the middle and top, and then enhance the top with the most luscious, juicy, bright red ones that you have saved for this purpose.

★

## Fig Shortcake

Do not lose sight of the delectableness of a fresh fig shortcake. Peel and slice the figs, cover with sugar and mash. Fill the cake with crushed figs, put some on top, and decorate with some whole peeled ones as well. Pass good cream, neither too thick nor too thin.

★

## Strawberries Romanoff

2 quarts beautiful strawberries, sugared
1 pint whipping cream
1 pint vanilla ice cream
2 ounces Cointreau
1 ounce rum
Juice of 1 lemon

Put the berries in the bottom of a large handsome bowl. Whip the vanilla ice cream slightly and fold in the whipped cream, adding the liqueurs and lemon juice. Pour this mixture over the berries. Serves six.

Mrs. James Bodrero of San Francisco substitutes cream cheese for the ice cream, using plenty of powdered sugar and enough thick cream to soften the cheese.

In a large quantity, this is a very good idea for a buffet supper.

★

## Trèfle

A recipe from the cookbook of the Comtesse de Vignerole, of Paris.

Arrange a layer of lady fingers or macaroons in a bowl or mold. Cover with puréed apricot jam, then cover with another layer of cakes. Cover with crème pâtissière, then top with a third layer of cakes that have been soaked in rum. Chill in refrigerator, turn out on a platter, and top with crème pâtissière. Decorate top with sweetened whipped cream, using a pastry tube.

★ NOTE: *A French version of the famous English dessert trifle.* H.E.B.

★

## Floating Island

This is a capital dessert. Beat 3 egg whites stiff, and gradually beat in ⅛ cup of sugar. Heat 2 cups of milk in a skillet, and drop tablespoons of the meringue mixture into it to poach. When set, lift out with a draining spoon and place on top of a dish of crème Anglaise made from recipe on page 194. Serves six.

# Glossary

AU GRATIN. Topped with crumbs or cheese (or both) and browned in the oven or under the broiler.

BAIN-MARIE. A receptacle containing water, warm but not boiling, in which is placed a second pan or saucepan, or molds, containing the food to be cooked. The hot water should be about halfway up the side of the cooking dish. This method makes for gentler cooking, and also keeps ingredients from overcooking or burning on direct flame. It is also used to keep already prepared dishes warm until serving time.

BARD. Thin slices of salt or fresh pork fat laid over meat or poultry before cooking.

BARQUETTE. Boat-shaped pastries or toast for various fillings.

BEURRE MANIÉ (kneaded butter). Equal parts of butter and flour, kneaded together until smooth. Useful when formed into small balls and added to liquid for thickening purposes. It will keep well in the refrigerator, and freezes beautifully.

CASSEROLE. A dish for baking, often of earthenware, usually with a cover.

CHARLOTTE. A round tin cake mold. It often has fluted sides, and the top is somewhat larger in circumference than the bottom.

COCOTTE. A small covered casserole usually used for a whole fowl or one piece of meat.

COURT BOUILLON. Liquid for poaching fish, shellfish, and sometimes meat. A good recipe is a quart of water (half may be white wine), 1 onion stuck with 2 cloves, an herb bouquet, 2 carrots, 2 celery ribs, and, if available, 2 leeks. Simmer for an hour, strain, and use as directed in the recipe. If no wine is used, it is advisable to add 2 or 3 tablespoons of vinegar.

DARIOLES. Ramekins; small cups. Darioles are usually made of tin, a little deeper than ramekins, which are usually made of porcelain. Used for individual custards, egg dishes, etc.

ÉCHALOTE. Shallot; small red-, brown-, or purple-skinned bulb of the onion family, with a slight flavor of garlic.

EN DÔME. In a dome-shaped mound.

ESCALOPES. Thin slices of veal, flattened with a mallet.

FINES HERBES. Herbs, finely minced . . . parsley, celery leaves, tarragon, chervil, chives, and so on. Includes, too, rosemary, sage, thyme, and the like.

GIGOT. The French word for leg of lamb, mutton, or venison.

GLACE DE VIANDE. This is meat glaze, useful for adding richness to soups and sauces. If you can't find it in your local fancy food store, use bouillon cubes or, preferably, simmer bouillon until it has been reduced to a thick jelly. This will keep almost indefinitely in a covered jar in the refrigerator.

HERB BOUQUET (bouquet garni). A small bunch of herbs, tied with a string (or wrapped in a small piece of cheesecloth, if dried herbs are used), for seasoning soups and sauces. Usually consists of 2 or 3 sprigs of parsley, a bay leaf, and a sprig of thyme, though other herbs are often added.

HERBS. Unless otherwise specified, the herbs used in this book are fresh ones. If dried herbs must be substituted, cut the amount by one-half. If you have any garden space at all, reserve one corner for herbs — tarragon, parsley, chives, chervil, thyme, etc. There are shops in large cities where fresh herbs are procurable, as well as several excellent brands of dried herbs. Learn to use herbs and to appreciate them. Try an herb window box, *faute de mieux*.

JULIENNE. To cut julienne is to cut in uniform slivers, like enlarged matches.

MARKETING. If you aim to have a creditable table, *do your own marketing!* (Unless you have that rara avis, a treasure of a cook!)

Pick out everything yourself. Don't order by telephone unless you have, and equally rare, a store that specializes in service.

MUSHROOMS. Never peel mushrooms. Don't let them stand in water. Either wash each one carefully under a tap, wiping them at once on a dry cloth, or wash them collectively in a saucepan, working quickly. To peel them is to lose much of their taste, just as soaking them ruins flavor and makes them soggy.

ORANGES. To cut properly: pierce one end of the orange with a large fork — one from the carving set is excellent. Select the sharpest knife you own. Make a circular incision around the base of the fruit, near the fork, cutting through the peel to the flesh. Then, from the top, cut down through the peel toward the fork. Cut into peel to reveal the flesh completely free of pith. You will end up with an orange-colored globe. Now cut, with minute precision, the flesh adhering to the segment on either side. Let the morsel fall into an awaiting bowl. Continue until you have the orange's skeleton impaled on the fork, and the dish filled with beautiful segments. I took a lesson in doing this from Robert, maître d'hôtel at the Paris Ritz.

PAPILLOTE. A paper covering, wrapped around fish, flesh, or fowl before baking, or sometimes frying. This method produces a greater degree of heat, and seals in all the juices. Use parchment or bond paper or foil, and double-fold the edges. Serve in the papers, which have been cut open with sharp scissors.

RAVIER. Hors d'oeuvre dish.

ROUX. A mixture of flour and butter as a base for sauce. White roux is not browned; for a brown roux, the flour is allowed to take color in the saucepan before the butter is incorporated. Later on, for a sauce, comes the bouillon, water, milk, or cream.

SAUTÉ. To stew gently in butter, as opposed to frying. And please pronounce it *so*-tay and NOT *saw*-tay.

SUPRÊME. A word used in France for the breast of a fowl.

TAMMY. A sieve; in French, "passoire." Fine or coarse; sometimes a cheesecloth answers the purpose.

*L'Envoi*

They dined on mince and slices of quince,
Which they ate with a runcible spoon.

— EDWARD LEAR

# Index

[ 232 ]

[ 234 ]

[ 236 ]